BOY

BYE!

VOLUME 2

BOY

BYE!

VOLUME 2

NO MORE RIDE OR DIE

Ride or die: The highest level of loyalty.

But if you've gotta *die* to stay on the ride,
that's a red flag and a sign to RUN!

Table of Contents

The following brave women are the contributing authors to this book and the collective healing journey:

Andrea Madison

Arieka S. Epkins

Barbara E. Thomas

Camile Jené

Cherelle Lenise

Chetera Marie

Dionne M. Pringle

Haleigh Mull

Lisa Jean

Maya Johnson Cotton

Mel Holley

Melissa McGill

Nykol Island

Savannah West

Stacey Bleeker

Valerie Scott

"Being alone may scare you, but being in a bad relationship may damage you."

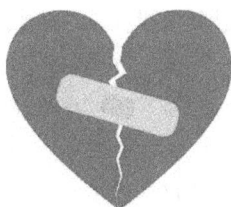

Journey 1

Like a Greek God

The sex was so good. He was blessed with a manhood of the right length and girth, and he knew how to use it to pleasure me immensely. He was doing things to my body that made my toes curl.

He took his time kissing and teasing my sweet spot with his tongue until she was super moist. The orgasms were powerful. Yet, something was missing. After the ecstasy faded, I wondered how I got into that space of numbness and despair. It was an empty mental space outside of the great sex, which eventually also became null and void.

Looking back on it, I thought I won the grand prize when I entered into a quick and monogamous relationship with him. After all, he was everything I asked for physically: Tall, dark, handsome, and had beautiful locs of hair. At 6 foot 6, he towered over me like a statue of a Greek god. His broad shoulders, muscular chest, and strong wide back alone made women stare. He had the perfectly sculptured washboard abs, with the sexy cut right above his massive penis. When he wore gray sweatpants, the package of his manliness could not help but be noticed. His thick black eyelashes and eyebrows sat upon a chiseled face like it had been shaped by Adonis himself. He was pleasing to the eyes. Still, I felt so alone, so disappointed and it wasn't long before I was seeking a different type of comfort.

The day he approached me, I was captivated by his appearance. He was a beautiful specimen to look at and his mannerisms matched. He was polite and funny. For a moment, I had to breathe just to make sure I wasn't hallucinating. I was walking out of a department store when this tall and gorgeous man walked up beside me.

"Hello, Ms. Lady. I don't mean to startle you or anything, but I am wondering if I can talk to you for a minute?" he said to me.

"Sure, but I am kind of in a hurry," I said trying not to blush at the sight of him.

He said, "I hope I don't offend you, but you are the most beautiful and sexy woman I have ever seen! Are you single or seeing anyone?"

I was definitely single and had almost given up on love finding me at that time in my life. I had gone through some bad relationships and decided to just focus on myself. I told God what I thought I wanted in a man, and I was waiting for that man to manifest. (Note to self: I should've waited...more to follow).

"Thank you for the compliment and yes, I am completely single," I said.

"Thank God! I would love to call you and take you out sometime if you would allow me to," he said.

Heck yes, I would allow him to call me! I had to

know more about this man. We exchanged pleasantries and phone numbers. I could not help but notice how he looked directly into my eyes when I was talking as if I had his full attention. Maybe, just maybe this would be "The One!"

RED FLAGS EVERYWHERE

Several weeks passed with us talking over the phone, texting each other every day, and going out on dates. For his size and stature, he was a gentle giant. He opened doors for me, held my hand when we walked together and showed so much chivalry. He would pull me close when other men were around and when he noticed other men looking. I thought this was a cute display of affection.

Our conversations were profound and intellectual. We talked about the wonders of the world but had different opinions on most things. I did not mind this at first because I like a man who can think for himself. He did not have a solid relationship with his mother but was fond of his grandmother. This was okay with me because I had specifically asked God for a man whose mother was not in the picture. My past experiences with a mama's boy tainted my perception of the mother-son relationship and I honestly did not want to deal with that again. He believed that family should not interfere with a couple's relationship. I could dig that too but to what extent remained to be seen.

We talked about our goals in life which seemed to be on different levels. I was living in a house I bought that was more like a starter home. I wanted a bigger house that I could make my dream home.

As we were discussing this one evening, he said, "Why do you want something so big when there's nothing wrong with what you have?"

My dream was slightly crushed, and I could not fathom why this man could not see beyond the now. I chalked it up to our backgrounds and how we were raised differently. I was not going to try and change his mind, nor would I change my mind. After all, we were still in the early stages of dating.

The first time we had sex, it was like an explosion of ecstasy! He knew exactly what to do to make sure I reached an orgasm several times before he did. He told me he wanted to be so far inside me and so close to me that our smells became one. Creepy right?

He would call me during the day and tell me he could still smell my sweet cum on his body from the night before and did not want to share that smell with anyone else, ever. This man doted over me. He wanted me all to himself all the time. He was not afraid to give other men a look that read, *"She's mine so get to stepping bro."* He ignored other women who would either try to get his attention or simply smile at him. To him, we were the only ones in our little world.

INSECURITY

We committed to a relationship within a couple of months. We lived an hour away from each other at the time. He would tell me that he could not stand being so far away from me because if something happened to me, he could not be right there to protect me. He also talked about how he longed to be close to me every day. Against my better judgment, I allowed him to move in with me temporarily.

Although he began to talk about marriage and the future, I was not quite there yet. At that stage of my life, everything was about showing and proving, not just talking. Yet here we were now living together. The plan was that he would find a place of his own within 60 days. I was working two jobs, so I required him to have two jobs, too. Reluctantly, he agreed but made sure that I knew that he was not pleased with spending so much time apart from me.

Insecurity showed itself in the fish market. We went to a farmer's market to get groceries for dinner. I decided that I wanted fish. So, while he was browsing the aisles for other things, I went to the fish market. The sales guy asked me if he could help me. We discussed which fish was the freshest and would go well with the other items I planned to prepare. It was a basic fish conversation.

The sales guy prepared my purchase, handed it to me, smiled, and said, "Thank you for shopping with us today."

As I turned to walk away, my gorgeous man was standing there with this crazy look on his face.

"What the hell did he say to you?" he asked.

I was caught off guard and replied, "Who?!"

Surely he could not have been talking about the fish market sales guy.

"The dude in the fish market! I saw him smiling at you!"

I could not believe what I was hearing. I decided not to entertain it and instead stroked his ego a little.

"Aww babe, you know you're the only one for me. The sales guy was just being polite and trying to sell me some shrimp to go with the fish," I coyly said.

"I hope so because I told you that I do not want to share you with anyone else ever!" he said with a straight face.

On another occasion, I had an important project due at work. It required every staff member to stay late and work diligently on the project to meet the deadline. I called my gorgeous man from my desk phone to let him know that I was still at work and would be home late. I told him where the spare housekey was and to let himself him. Even though he had moved in with me, I had never given him a key to my house. He was only supposed to be there for 60 days anyway.

After working about 14 hours that day, I came home exhausted. All I wanted to do was take off my heels and clothes and take a long hot shower. I greeted my gorgeous man with a hug and a quick kiss. I went to the bedroom, tossed my heels and clothing on the chair, went into the bathroom, and let the lavender smell and hot water wash off the day's hustle and bustle.

I was drying off with a towel when I noticed the bathroom door ajar. I could see my gorgeous man sitting in the chair where I had tossed my clothing. I had to blink to make sure I was seeing what I was seeing. This man of mine had my underwear under his nose inhaling deeply. I put on my robe and went into the bedroom to find out what was going on. He said that our smell had been tainted because he could smell another man's semen in my underwear. I was flabbergasted! I also was angry!

I had just left work and came straight home. I also called him from my desk phone to let him know that I was working late and a few more times after that so he would not worry. That night was the first of many arguments about his insecurity.

MIGHT AS WELL HAD CHEATED ON YOU

I was constantly being accused of cheating. Each time we had sex he would request that I say things like "*I promise this pu*** is all yours,*" and ask me to say his name. He wanted to control what I wore including my lingerie. The accusations were getting out of hand. I felt so heavy and uncomfortable.

For my efforts in getting a project completed at work, I earned a free trip to a beautiful city out west. The hotel was 5-star with rooms starting at about $800.00 a night. I asked for accommodations to take my gorgeous man with me so that he could see that I was not cheating on him. The trip was disastrous. I got accused of flirting with the bartender, the bellhop, the valet guy, and any other man we encountered.

On a separate occasion, we went to visit my college friends (husband and wife) for a weekend getaway. We were at a bar, laughing and reminiscing about our college days. My guy friend mentioned how I used to be the cherry stem tongue-tying champ. For fun, I wanted to see if I could still do it. My guy friend and I raced to get a cherry in our mouths to see who could tie the stem first. I won! However, my gorgeous man was not impressed. Later that night, he accused me of sucking my guy friend's penis. That was it! I had had enough of his insecurity and accusations. I began to look at him differently that night and had to find a way out of the space he put me in.

SELF RIGHTEOUS B***H

What I had come to realize was that I was in a relationship with a tall, dark, and handsome physical specimen of a man with no substance inside. Even the sex became boring. It was no longer enough to fill the void I had in my life. I needed more than a physical relationship. I wanted someone who believed in themselves, had high hopes and aspirations, was not dependent on me, and most of all was confident.

Jealousy and insecurity had been a stalemate in this relationship. Not only was my man jealous of other men, but he was also jealous of my relationship with my family. Whenever my family would come over, he would fake like he was sick so that they'd leave. He would continuously smell my underwear to see if he could smell another man's semen. He would go through my phone when I wasn't looking. I had a phone that disappeared and to this day, I think he destroyed it because there were old pictures of guy friends in it.

The day I put this gorgeous yet broken man out of my house was momentous. We were playing spades with my family members. My man reneged and when my family called it, he was upset that I didn't take his side. The argument went from spades to "you must've f****d them too!" I stood up immediately and told him to get his things and get out of my house.

On his way out the door, the last thing he said to me was, "You're a self-righteous b***h!"

My reply, "Boy BYE! Next!"

"It is better for someone to break your heart once by leaving your life, than for them to stay in your life and break your heart continually."

Journey 2

A Dream Derailed

So, just how desperate are you? How important is it for you to experience TRUE LOVE? HALF ASS LOVE? A PIECE OF LOVE? THAT WHICH POSSESSES THE ESSENCE OF LOVE, BUT UNDENIABLY, IS NOT LOVE? When do you decide that ALL the red flags matter and not one should be overlooked? When do you begin to adhere to the counsel that you so graciously dispense to others? Well, honestly, it took me out, but I got there. I had to tell this Boy, BYE!

Whew! Lawd knows that I love a husky and muscular, tall, dark chocolate, intelligent, sexy, beautiful bright white smile, and delightful smelling black man. Baby, there's none greater! They are truly my kryptonite. I guess the devil knew that too. Here I was at the local carwash minding my business and this man walked over and sat by me on the bench. I almost passed out from the heat my body started generating. Somehow a nice 75-degree day turned into a California, High Desert 110 and burning situation. I'm not gonna lie, my immediate thoughts were of FIRE and DESIRE. I had a thousand and one thoughts of exactly what I wanted to experience with this man. I mean, am I wrong? How often do you come across a 6'4" man with big feet and hands who possesses the essence of a God?

"Hello beautiful! How are you?" he said, as he completely melted me.

I smiled and responded with a shy, "Hi. I'm well, thank you."

Oh, I tried my best to keep it together while answering his question.

"It's burning up out here!" I began pointing out the changes in temperature hoping he wouldn't realize all the sweat running down my cleavage.

DAMN! My hormones were in overdrive and that wasn't cool.

As I casually took some tissue from my purse and dabbed my chest, I'm grateful that he didn't make mention of it at all. We were hitting it off great.

The hour it usually takes for them to wash my car flew by so fast. Talk about feeling as if you've known someone from a previous life is an understatement. This man had my full attention, and I was stuck. His root beer brown eyes had me locked in. The fact that he was intelligent, successful, and thoughtful lured me deeper. Did I mention his smile? Of course I did!

By the time my car was ready, we had consummated such an exquisite conversation that neither one of us was ready to abandon it. I felt as if he were playing the piano and I was floating on every note as I sang "The Very Thought Of You" by the incomparable Ella Fitzgerald. There was something extremely exceptional here. However, I can be shy, and I need an assertive man. If a man doesn't ask for the number then he just won't get it. OLD SCHOOL CHIVALRY IS IMPORTANT TO ME!

As the carwash worker waved to me for the second time, I started gathering my things so I could leave.

When I stood up, I told this fine man next to me, "It was nice conversing with you. Have an excellent day!"

Flashing that billion-dollar smile, he said, "How are you going to leave without exchanging numbers with me? You didn't enjoy our conversation?"

I'm sure that my tight eyes bucked wide open.

"Of course I did!" I said, as he grabbed my hand.

"I'm King. It's a pleasure to meet you miss..."

Baaaby! Didn't he feel that? I was already pregnant from my thoughts and his touch!

"Kola. I'm Kola. It's been a pleasure, King."

We exchanged numbers and he walked me to my car.

King opened the car door, and I said, "Thank you sweetheart!" and got in.

As soon as that door closed, my car became a confession box and I started praying because "FATHER, I HAVE SINNED!"

My whole drive home was full of prayer. Ya girl had to ensure that I wasn't going to be engulfed in his physique and a deep conversation.

Later that night, King called me. I knew it was already late in the evening. I looked at the time, a little after 9 p.m., and thought that I'd call him in the morning. You see, I was raised in a household where all calls stopped after 9 p.m. If someone was calling that late then it better be an emergency. It was a respect thing. This worked great for me because after all that praying earlier,

I would've lost myself with that baritone voice in my ear as I was lying in bed.

First thing in the morning, I sent King a short text letting him know that I'm usually asleep before 9 p.m. and that he could give me a call before we both headed in to work. To my surprise, he called right away.

King told me that he was off on Fridays and was hoping that he could take me to breakfast that morning. I informed him that I wasn't off. His response shocked me.

"I know you aren't. Call off and I'll give you your full pay for the day."

I seriously sat there and rolled my eyes. A plethora of thoughts, comments, and concerns flooded my brain. I understood he was a business owner and was well off. However, he didn't know what I made in a day. I felt like that was so intrusive and that he was doing the most. How often is this charm and employment wage going out the door to get what he wanted?

I responded, "No! I'm not calling off to go to breakfast. That's crazy! We can see one another sometime this weekend."

This made me think this man was so into himself. He knew he was fine and was probably used to getting his way.

He said, "You're not just taking off to go to breakfast. You're taking off to spend time with your future!"

OH, MY GOODNESS! WHERE did this man come from? See when you're used to getting the short end of the stick because you're so loving and giving, it's hard to be open to accepting what could be genuine sometimes.

I decided to take a chance on love and go to breakfast. What could it hurt? I wasn't losing out on anything since I was still getting my wages for the day.

King came and picked me up looking and smelling amazing! Gazing into his pretty brown eyes just whipped me all over again.

"So, where would you like to go?" King asked.

We hadn't conversed about where we were going for breakfast which was weird. I believe we both were more concerned about seeing one another again than anything else. I asked King what his favorite breakfast restaurant was and told him that I'd like to go there. I really wanted to watch him dine on his favorite dishes so I could observe him. I was in study mode.

Everything about this man was nothing short of amazing. It all seemed too good to be true and you know what they say about that. If it seems too good to be true, then more than likely it is.

I was pushing to stay on the positive side of things. King said that his favorite restaurant was the Grand Lux in Beverly Hills. I was excited because I had never been there. I heard that the food was good, and this was where all the ballers ate.

When we arrived, all of the luxury cars were valeted where they could be seen. It was nice. Of course, King was having his Benz parked by valet as well. I, on the other hand, was more excited to go inside and watch him eat.

As we walked through the doors, King was greeted by name and was asked if he would like to be seated at his regular table.

"Of course," he responded.

King was a gentleman and I loved that. He pulled out my chair and asked if I liked where we were seated.

I responded, "This is fine."

I was ready to dig into his business now. Not only was it his favorite restaurant, but he was a regular.

King ordered us a bottle of champagne as I looked over the menu. We ordered our food, and I began asking questions. I had to know if I really did call off work to sit in the presence of all that I had prayed for.

Every answer that King gave was right up my alley. He was single, had no kids, and was in search of his queen. We discussed what we desired for the future and those things went hand in hand. King was a God sent man!

After breakfast, we spent a little time at Santa Monica pier playing some of the games and enjoying what seemed to be a complete blessing in disguise. I was so elated that I had taken a leap of faith! What an excellent day it was to be out, feeling free, and enjoying life.

Time passed so quickly, and I noticed it was time to pick up my child. I really wasn't ready to leave King. Our conversation deepened as we headed to my home. Again, that place of comfort was present that I worried about.

When we arrived at my place, King walked me to my door. He asked when he could see me again as he handed me some neatly folded bills. Grinning from ear to ear, I told him that we'd figure it out soon and that I needed to pick up my son.

He grabbed me and hugged me tight, kissed my forehead and said, "Ok beautiful. Drive safe and let me know when you make it back home."

Look here y'all! I walked into my house and almost forgot that I needed to leave. That kiss on my forehead was so soft and kind. What was I feeling and why so early?

I realized I had money in my hand and opened it up. It was $500 and a small sticky note that read "Thank you for choosing me today!"

One day of skipping work and taking a chance on love turned into almost two years of bliss. How much higher could I get off of this man's love? King and my son were my world! There was never any drama or disrespect and we rarely disagreed about anything. King would often speak to me about marriage and what our future would look like. He wanted to start a family and grow old together. I was in awe of what I was experiencing. King was PERFECT for me and my child! We really took care of each other.

***

Our anniversary was coming up and we had planned a wonderful trip to Jamaica. We were both excited about just being able to get away and relax. On this particular hot summer day, King was headed to the Burbank office, and I was off for the day. I took my child to school and was happy that I could just chill and relax for the most part. My plans were to stop by the store and grab all the ingredients to make King's favorite meal, do some dusting and relax.

I began preparing our dinner around 3:30 p.m. when a call came through to my phone that I didn't recognize. I waited to see if they were going to leave a message. They did not. I left and picked up my son around 4 p.m., made it back home by 5 p.m., checked to see how much time was needed for my food, spent some time with my child and awaited the arrival of my King.

As I was in the kitchen singing Anita Baker's "Whatever It Takes" to the top of my lungs, the phone rang. It was Ms. Juanita, King's mother.

"Hey momma!" Ms. Juanita's voice was low.

"Something happened while King was at work and he won't be coming home tonight."

I screamed!

Then, I heard her voice say, "He's ok. I just need you to come over so we can talk about what's going on."

My heart was now in my ass! I was trying to figure out what could've occurred. What did she mean by my baby wasn't coming home?

I dropped my son off to my parents and drove to Ms. Juanita's house. When I arrived, there was a lady I'd never seen before sitting on the couch and twin boys who looked a little older than my son running around.

"Hi baby," Ms. Juanita said.

"Come and have a seat."

As I sat at the edge of the recliner, she began to speak.

"Well, I called you both here to let you know that King has been taken in for fraud."

Whose King? NOT *MY* KING! Not the man I was supposed to spend the rest of my life with?

"Kola, he tried to call you earlier because he wanted to explain some things to you. Now, I have to explain."

As I'm boo hoo crying, I noticed the lady on the couch seemed to not be fazed by any of the news.

"That's Tasha, King's wife, and his boy's, Deshaun and Dezmond."

I screamed the loudest!

"HIS WHAT?!" from the bottom of my soul.

Here I was in love with a complete fraud. Where had this wife and kids been for two years and why were they kept a secret...not just by King but his momma too? I felt like I had been doused with gasoline because I was hot!

In the midst of Ms., Juanita trying to explain

everything to me, the random number pops up on my phone again. I answered and it was King. The sound of his voice made me realize how hurt I really was. I was devastated! How could he do this to me? My son? We were a family. I couldn't take it!

The words coming out of his mouth no longer held weight. I cursed him out and told him how raggedy he and his mother were. I hung up in his face and left out of Ms. Juanita's home in a rage. When I got in my car, I broke down! Two years of happy memories were now pieces of shattered glass jarring through me. Once I finally made it home, I cried myself to sleep.

King went to prison. I refused to answer his phone calls or respond to his mailed letters. What would make him think that I could talk to him after the level of deception he pulled? I lost my FOREVER. I was messed up and Ms. Juanita didn't make it any better. She would come by my house and put envelopes of money in my mailbox with writing on the front that read "FROM KING! ANSWER HIS CALL!"

That love and desperation that I had for King had died. I was living a dream that had now turned into me riding on a bus with Freddy Krugger. Ugh! I should've just gone to work, dammit!

***Stormy Weather by Etta James
***You Ain't Sh*t by Riskay

"Bravery is leaving a toxic relationship and knowing that you deserve better."

Journey 3

Untitled

I learned a lot from watching others and knew my worth at a young age. I made the conscious decision not to have a boyfriend while I was in high school. Getting through school was my focus. I didn't want any distractions that could hinder me. I saw how it affected others.

I watched one of my friends lose who she was just to say she had a boyfriend. It was so important to her to the point she started losing her way. Her grades even started slipping.

Another friend was in an abusive relationship, and another one was pregnant and eventually dropped out of high school. I watched them make poor choices time after time and I didn't want to follow suit. I knew early on that I would never put up with the mess my friends put up with.

I was fresh out of high school at 17 and not old enough to go to the clubs. My friends were of age and could go, and they would have the security guard let me in the back entrance. I had male friends, but no one I would call my boyfriend. We would hang out and sometimes we would all go out in groups. We all loved to dance and went out as often as we could. There were several 21 and over clubs, but not too many 18 and over. We had NTC-Navel Training Center which was probably one of the favorite spots, MCRD, City College, and a couple more.

One evening, I met someone at NTC. I saw him out a few times and I thought to myself he was good-looking. On one particular evening, he approached me and asked me to dance. After the song was over, I started to walk away, and he grabbed my hand to continue dancing. Eventually, I was tired and needed a break. He followed and we sat and talked. We exchanged phone numbers and that's when the friendship started.

He was in the military in Oceanside, which was approximately a 30 to 40-minute drive for him. But he was always in San Diego, so it was no big deal. We would hang out and go to the movies, walk the beach, go bike riding, and roller skating. We had a lot of fun together. He was a few years older than me, and what I really liked is he was a gentleman. He would hold my hand, open doors, and was just a good person. I couldn't ask for more and he checked off most of the boxes.

A month or so into the friendship, he wanted to date exclusively and asked me to be his girlfriend, but I said no. I didn't want to rush anything, and he said he understood. We continued to hang out.

One evening, we were going to the movies. He picked me up and handed me a dozen beautiful pink roses. He always brought me flowers. I was so lucky to have met such a great guy. I wasn't in love but if this was really who he was it would have been easy to fall in love with him.

We had a very nice dinner, then we left, went to the movies, and had a good evening. He took me home and was very respectful at the door. We got to the point where we would see each other often, and it was always a good time.

One evening we had plans to go see a play and of course, dinner was involved. During dinner, he talked about being in a relationship with me. He expressed that he could see us one day getting married as he rambled about the future. I had to put a stop to that because for me he was moving way too fast. Most importantly, I was not in love, but I liked him a lot. Love would come naturally; I just wasn't there yet.

He told me he wasn't used to being told no and that it was a hard pill to swallow. I simply told him I wasn't ready for what he presented, and he needed to slow down. Talking about marriage was a deal breaker. I told him at that time in my life marriage wasn't even in the same city as me. I could tell that irritated him by the look on his face. I saw something I hadn't seen before which was a bit of an attitude, but I didn't say anything.

As the evening progressed, he got very quiet and showed a different side of himself. I kept asking him what was wrong, but he just shut down. So, I shut down as well. After the play was over, he took me home and barely said goodbye.

That following week I only heard from him once and it was a brief conversation. The week after that he reached out, but I didn't respond because I was busy and went out of town. I heard he had called a few times for me, and I didn't see a need to return his call because I felt he needed time to himself. I returned home that Sunday, and Monday evening he had the nerve to just show up which wasn't cool. I had my mom get rid of him by telling him I wasn't home.

The very next day I received flowers and a note. He wanted to go out to brunch and talk, which was fine with me, so I agreed to go. This time I met him at the restaurant just in case he wanted to act a fool I could leave in my own vehicle. He started the conversation but couldn't focus on me his eyes were all over the place. He was checking out other women, dang near gawking at every female that walked past. I thought it was rude and disrespectful. Again, I was seeing a different side of this person. I didn't have a lot of tolerance for mess, but I certainly knew what was acceptable for me, and in that moment his actions were not.

Those who knew me were aware that I was very shy and quiet, but I was not going to let that slide. Again, I knew my worth and what I wasn't going to put up with. I told him he was being disrespectful, and he had the nerve to tell me we weren't in a relationship, so he wasn't doing anything wrong by looking. Oh, I see now.

Slowly the layers were coming off and I made sure not to miss a thing. He didn't know who he was dealing with. I asked him how he would feel if I did the same thing, and he said he didn't care because he was confident in himself. I said ok and laughed. We finished dinner and called it an evening.

The next couple of weeks I was busy and didn't make myself available to even hang out with him as he had shown me a side of him that wasn't ok with me. I needed to step back. See, this is the very reason why I wanted to wait and not rush into anything.

Over time we started hanging out again. One weekend we went bike riding at the beach. While riding bikes he was clearly rusty and at one point his bike hit mine. I lost my balance. I wasn't hurt but he thought it was funny. A stranger stopped to help me to my feet. He jumped off his bike, pushed me aside to try to flex his muscles telling the guy to take his hands off me. First, he messed up by pushing me aside. My reaction was to push back, and I did. I looked at him and asked him if he had lost his mind. He claimed that was an accident. The nice guy who helped me stood at my side just in case. Everything turned out fine, but I had made up my mind regarding him. Again, I saw another side of this person which wasn't ok.

At that point, I was ready to go home. On the drive, he accused me of flirting with that guy and I told him I wasn't flirting and that he needed to grow up. He raised his voice at me, and I told him I wasn't his child, and I wouldn't stand for it. He apologized but it fell on death's ears as far as I was concerned.

One weekend, I hung out with some girlfriends, and we ended up at the NTC to go dancing. Lo and behold, I saw him out of the corner of my eye on the dance floor getting down with a female. The only problem was they probably should have gotten a room. It was that nasty! All eyes were on them.

I got on that dance floor and danced my way over to them. When he looked up and saw me dancing with a guy he did a double take and tried to pull me over to his side. I pushed back and he walked off the dance floor. I just kept dancing until I was tired.

After a couple of songs, I went to sit down and the guy I was dancing with followed and sat down, too. We talked a little and went our separate ways. The rest of the evening went well with no issues, but my guard was up.

The guy I was dancing with found me a little later in the evening and told me my boyfriend tried to confront him and had a few choice words to stay away from me. I told him this was not my boyfriend, just someone I was hanging out with, but we had no specific title just friends. Before the night was over I ran into him again and he grabbed me to try and pull me in, but I was stronger than he thought.

My mom always told me not to ever let a man put his hands on me. She said if one does I had better go for the family jewels, grab something, and knock his butt out. So, you know what I did. Yes I took my knee and went in as hard as I could, and he hit the floor. I wasn't worried about retaliation because I had back up which was a group of guys standing by ready to take of business.

I walked away, found my friends, and left the building. A couple of days later he called me to apologize saying that wasn't him and that he had too much to drink. Now mind you all the times we went out I never saw him with a drink. Now all of a sudden it wasn't him and it was the alcohol, right?

I was upset that I had wasted time with him, and as time went on feelings were involved. I knew what I had to do. He contacted me a few days later and wanted to meet. I didn't trust him, so I agreed to meet him at a restaurant where there was a crowd. We met up, I listened to what he had to say, all the begging and groveling. I could hardly stand it because I felt like it was all lies.

I had already made up my mind that it was time to move on; I didn't even want to be friends. When I'm done, I'm done. He told me that I was supposed to be his girl and one day his wife. I told him he was mistaken and that I clearly was not on the same page. He asked me to give him more time to prove himself and I told him no. He started to get a little loud and obnoxious. I got up, told him to have a good life, and I walked away with my dignity. As I walked away, he said he wouldn't let anyone else have me.

I heard what he said but I showed no reaction. I just kept walking until I reached the front door and walked briskly to my car. I was a little shaken up to hear his comment, but I knew I had made the right decision.

I never told anyone that he had basically threatened me. He kept calling until I told him again the friendship was over and to lose my number. Eventually he got the message.

I was sad, upset, and mad all at the same time. I felt like I was deceived. He was good at trying to hide who he actually was. I could not be too hard on myself, however because I didn't fall for him.

I stopped going out for a while, but at some point, I couldn't let him control my life by hiding. When I started going back out, I ran into him. I was out with a male friend who didn't leave my side, so it worked out. He watched me but did not approach me. At some point, I went to the ladies' room and when I came out there he was. Again, he tried pulling me towards him and my superhero stepped in right on time. I told him loud and clear he was crazy and that I never wanted to see or speak to him again.

I know he was embarrassed because he took off towards the front entrance. The next day, he showed up at my place, and my mom met him at the door. She told him not to come to her front door again or we would file a police report. Because he was in the military, they took care of everything, and he finally stopped bothering me.

Ladies, you should know your worth, what you will put up with, and what you won't put up with and stick to it. Don't settle just to say you have a boyfriend, or husband, because in the long run it will not work. It may hurt in the beginning, however the hurt and pain doesn't last always. When someone shows you who they are, please believe them. Run, don't walk away because it is not worth losing yourself or perhaps losing your life.

"No partner in a love relationship... should feel that he has to give up an essential part of himself to make it viable."

Journey 4

Narcissism No More

It all started in 2002. I began a job as a temp worker doing administrative work for a sheet metal company. It wasn't long after that I met the logistics manager, a charming, friendly man who made me laugh, consistently. He made a point to come and say good morning every day. He went out of his way to pay attention to me, surprised me with little gifts, played pranks on me, called me on my phone pretending to be someone else, just to get a reaction out of me. He loved to see me smiling and happy. He did all this when all the while he had a girlfriend at home. Red flag, right? It was, but I, being insecure in who God created me to be, ignored it. It felt good, it fed my insecurities, so I embraced and welcomed his advances, effort, and attention.

Years went by. We had established a solid friendship. We had also established late-night love sessions. They were different, he was different. He was there for me like none other. He was a shoulder to cry on, a gentle soul that appeared even tempered, and he was willing to sacrifice time with his family at home to do things & spend time with me. It was the little things that drew me in, such as my favorite kind of gum. He knew what it was, remembered, and bought it for me frequently.

Fast forward to 2011. Things between him and his girlfriend finally fell apart. His "main" finally saw the light. Nine years of prayers had finally been answered. I had him all to myself.

She couldn't ignore the chemistry between us any longer. It was in fact undeniable when we were together. Years of being invited to all their house parties; the way he looked after me in front her, the late nights in my bed while her kids were calling him wondering where he was at, the many days he had to "work late" while we spent hours at the park sipping on anything & everything. The law even showed up on us one night, our shenanigans almost landed us in jail. In fact, confusion sets in when I think about how blinded to our "love" she was for so long.

The red flags were many. However, I ignored every single one, to the point that we moved to Arizona together, from Georgia, in 2012. We got married one year to the day later after being pressured by our church, after finding out I was pregnant with our son. That's when things really began to unfold for the worse.

It was February 24, 2014, the day our son was born.

His first comment when the doctor pulled him out of my belly was, "He's mighty white. Are you sure he doesn't belong to the mailman?"

My husband was African American and I'm as white

as snow. His genes were not prominent in our son, hence his comment. Our son has straight hair, like mine, his skin of lighter complexion.

His famous words when I question things that he'd say, "I was just joking" or "I can't say anything around you, you're so sensitive."

The fact that I didn't approve of every rude comment made him feel that he had to walk on eggshells around me. I quickly began to realize that he had been disguising his disrespectful ways.

As our son got older, it became very evident that our parenting personalities were at odds. He was quick to whip out the belt, while I found patience to be much more productive. This was the beginning of the end. I began to realize that our son had taken on my husband's aggressive tendencies. I knew you couldn't fight fire with fire, but my husband wasn't convinced. A whooping was all he knew. Two damaged bedroom doors later, I knew my son was quickly turning into a monster. His fits of rage, blacking out and not realizing moments later what he had just done, had me scared to death for his future.

I began a prayer journey with a good friend that lasted well over three years. Week after week, crying out in desperation to the Holy One of Israel, pleading for divine intervention, not just for my son but for my marriage, for my teenage daughter, for agreement, for unity. I was lost. I desperately wanted to be found.

We were in church, had exhausted our use of therapists, read books, went to every marriage class and event we could find. Twelve years later, change was as far off as it had ever been. I asked myself and God the hard things daily. Answers were absent. Conversations with my husband regarding the issues were at best....crazy and a complete waste of time. I was alone, alone with my thoughts, alone in my pain. Was depression trying to reel me back in?

Parenting became a responsibility that I resented. Why did I have to "deal" with my kids? I had no joy, energy, love, or peace. My heart had turned colder than an Alaskan winter. The critical remarks of my husband had turned my kids against me. Making meals became an ordeal that made me cringe. His first comment when walking through the door was a critical comment regarding my cooking procedures. It wasn't long before my daughter refused my meals. Chaos and confusion had become a norm in our house. His need to echo every word I said to the kids was justified by his so called "manhood." They need to hear it from a man otherwise they won't listen. I wasn't enough, my role as a mom ceased to exist.

Fast forward to August 2023. I left. I was done. There was no turning back. Come hell or high water, I was out. I had not settled on a divorce but at minimum we had to separate to make room for peace and clarity. It no longer mattered what people, pastors, friends, counselors said. I said BOY BYE, temporarily. I had embarrassed myself enough at the altar every Sunday, crying out for mercy, pleading for change that my husband was clearly not interested in. All of this happened in front of people who had given us "sound" advice, time and time again based on a fraction of our story.

His attempts at working on our marriage after the separation were just as nonexistent as they were when we were cohabitating. An occasional phone call at night to read a bible verse he had no interest in applying to our life and pray a prayer to check that off his to do list was the highlight of his efforts. Yet he somehow genuinely felt like he was doing his best, and most of all at the same time. What didn't change was his "man of God" behavior at church, and his worldly, selfish, loveless, treatment of me & our kids the moment we left the church parking lot.

Four months into the separation, sickness had also set in, again but on another level. Random burning and itching all over my body added yet another layer of struggle that I wasn't prepared for. B vitamins were the only thing that calmed the nerves, to a point. Perhaps there was a deficiency?

After seeing four doctors, determined to find a physical ailment of some sort, I was told, "Ma'am there's nothing wrong with you. You have a severe case of stress and anxiety."

My marriage was making me sick, literally. It was time, time too fast. I was desperate for direction. Something had to change. I cried out to God, AGAIN, but this was a different kind of cry. God responded and He spoke in ways I'd never heard him before.

1 Corinthians 7:15 – if the unbeliever leaves, let it be so. The brother or sister is not bound in such circumstances. God has called us to live in peace.

What? An unbeliever? But both my husband and I were in church. We were both believers, right? That's not what God said. God quickly brought me to the definition of believer. Faith is a synonym of belief, and faith requires action. My husband had been doing all the Christian "things," yet his actions away from the house of God in no way reflected that of a believer.

Amos 3:3 – how can two walk together unless they agree?

This was a no-brainer. We couldn't even agree on what to cook for dinner.

1 Corinthias 13:4 – love is patient, love is kind, it does not envy it does not boast, it is not proud.

Although I'm not a hero in my own story, I can say honestly, that I was patient with his blatant disregard of me. Twenty years patient as a matter of fact. I endured emotional abuse, abandonment, selfish motivation and decisions, loveless sex, a transactional relationship with someone I wanted desperately to grow up and see the light. I had moments of spiritual highs where I was as kind as kind could be despite the mistreatment. It was, however, not sustainable due to his ongoing lack of respect. I became unable to overcome his level of evil with good.

I just wanted to forgive and forget. I had a moment of forgiveness in church. I felt a huge weight lifted off. I had forgiven him, truly. Yet the struggle to forget was as real as it had ever been.

During one of hundreds of therapy sessions, I remember being told, "You can start healing once the bleeding stops."

How was the bleeding going to stop? We have kids to co-parent. As much as I just wanted to skip town and forget this entire chapter of my life, I knew that disappearing wasn't the answer. The fact remained; the bleeding had to stop.

As I prayed, "God help me to forget," the opposite happened. Everything I was hoping to forget was suddenly at the forefront of my mind. God needed to remind me so I wouldn't return to the strong trauma bond that needed to be broken. I was reminded of the sleepless nights, crying myself to sleep while he slept like a baby, not one bit concerned about me, or about us. The hurt, the tears that he blatantly ignored. The hours I spent crying in the closet, while he was laughing & playing basketball with our son were the worst. Our son cared enough to check on me while my husband just walked around the house like nothing was happening. Cold-hearted behavior and emotional abandonment were his expertise. The rude and critical comments on the way to church that left me begging for relief at the alter almost every single Sunday, while he handed me tissues acting concerned about me, the countless times he told me to just stop talking, the constant reminders that he didn't want to hear it, the lack of compassion and empathy, his ongoing need to drink alcohol to cope with his own issues, his selfish acts that were done all in the name of love, were in fact not love at all. God is love and if there is no love, there is no God. Conversations with him usually involved what's in it for him. I had to come to terms with the fact that the marriage I had fought so hard for was a fraud. I was fighting for a man who had zero interest in fighting for me.

He called me for prayer one random night during the separation and shared scriptures God had given him:

Job 11:13-18 – (New International Version) "Yet if you devote your heart to him and stretch out your hands to him, if you put away the sin that is in your hand and allow no evil to dwell in your tent, then, free of fault, you will lift up your face; you will stand firm and without fear. You will surely forget your trouble, recalling it only as waters gone by. Life will be brighter than noonday, and darkness will become like morning. You will be secure, because there is hope; you will look about you and take your rest in safety."

If God had given that to me, I'd have no choice to drop to my knees and repent. Did he? No! In fact, that was the last I heard of it. No response, no emotion, no repentance, no self-examination because surely God wouldn't be talking to him about him would he? His blatant disregard and disobedience to God's instruction was by far the most troublesome.

"There's a difference between difficult and destructive," stated a guest speaker on a radio show who had also recently divorced her toxic husband.

Marriage is difficult, but it should never be destructive. That sealed it for me. My marriage was destroying me and my children. I knew it was time to say BOY BYE. I was done fighting and he never started. Peace and clarity were foreigners. I needed to get reacquainted. I knew staying in a place of turmoil was not God's will for me, or my children. His plans for us are good, and not evil. (Jeremiah 29:11). All we knew was evil, it was time to experience good.

"When he's the last thing you need, he'll drain you. He'll exhaust you. He'll destroy you. And you won't see it that way. In fact, you won't notice it at all. But everyone else will."

Journey 5

Unfavorable Connection

How did I end up here? Marriage done for over two years. Divorce final. Coparenting. And still stuck. All in the name of people pleasing. Divorced, yet enmeshed and living with all of the stress of the marriage that nearly killed me. No! I had to break free.

Two sheltered young adults in their 20's embarked on what seemed to be a beautiful journey of love and triumph. We didn't know anything, so we discovered a lot together. We explored new things and were developing what I thought would equate to a beautiful life of joy, victory, family, and love that transcends the ups and downs of life.

It was very bumpy, and I covered a lot (kept everything like evictions, repossessions, no money for food, to myself) because I just knew that it would smooth out. Everyone around us championed our love story. Building careers, excelling, learning, growing in our relationships with God, loving through health challenges, and growing seemingly together. Then, a shift occurred.

What I thought was true love showed its true colors eventually.

Transactional love. What can you do for me? When my abilities — due to an ongoing health issue discovered pre-marriage — diminished and I was no longer seen to be as valuable as determined before, I became a burden. What I required moving forward as a woman and wife cost too much and I became expendable. And the worst part, I believed I deserved this treatment.

Much healing had to take place before I could see my worth again. I believed from the beginning of our marriage I wasn't worthy due to health issues discovered just before we said, "I do." And in the end, that sobering reality met me at the door. The exit from that marriage.

He filed. I fought. Until I realized I was being set free. What started off as bliss, ended up being a nightmare and the freedom and healing I experienced as the divorce became final shifted my life. It woke me up and catapulted me into discovering my greatness. But years later I still felt attached in some respects. And I needed to be completely free.

I was trying to keep the peace and still let him have the control he was used to. I let threats and intimidation cause me to back down and give in to demands with the children. I was keeping the peace for him, this man that discarded me and has no loyalty to me, while continuing to destroy myself. Unacceptable.

The truth is, we will always be connected because we share children and currently they are of rearing age. I have to speak to him and collaborate with him, but I owe him nothing. So how can you have peace while coparenting with someone you'd rather not associate with?

Admittedly, I did not grow up with boundaries. I did not understand what true boundaries were until my 30s. Exploring what boundaries work for me and learning how to effectively communicate have been a game changer. I no longer feel unsafe when communicating with my children's father because I have taught him how to treat me. I have to keep it short and keep emotions out. My focus is on what is best for the children. Once I adopted this stance and learned how to keep my long responses at minimum, I effectively was able to yell, BOY BYE in my heart and mind while communicating with him with ease. Discovering this balance has been such a joy inducer for me. His text messages and calls no longer set me on edge because he can't control me any longer.

I want to encourage those who still have to be in contact with your ex. You can see them every week. Text them every day if need be, yet still proclaim, BOY BYE. For us it's more of a heart posture, but the refrain still remains.

"Know your worth and please don't invest in toxic people or relationships, because any bond that requires servicing is not worth your time."

Journey 6

The Abuser

I was getting off work one day and I noticed a black car sitting right on the side of my building. There was a very handsome gentleman sitting in a really nice BMW. You know, when women see these fly cars and good-looking men we have to do a double take.

So, as I began to walk towards my car, the BMW was driving up to the side of me. He looked over at my car and I got a little nervous because these days and back in those days you couldn't trust anyone rolling up on you.

The gentleman rolled his window down and said, "Hi, what's your name?"

I told him my name.

He said, "I am not trying to be rude but you're a very beautiful lady and I would like to know if you are involved with anyone?"

I looked over at him and said, "I am not involved with anyone at this time."

He chuckled and said, "You know what? I am a single male; you seem to be a single female. can we exchange numbers and maybe chat sometimes?"

I gave him my number and in about a day or two I received a call.

"Hi, this is Aldee. I met you at your office. I was just calling to say hi."

We engaged in a conversation. He told me a little bit about his life. He didn't have kids, he lived alone, and he had a decent job. I told him a little bit about myself. I told him I had a son and that I had been single for a while. We were both looking for a committed relationship. It was rare to find a man who was interested in being in a committed relationship.

A few days later, I got a call from him, but I was unable to answer, and he kept calling until I answered. That bothered me because he knew I was working during the hours he called. I should have paid attention to that. It was an early sign, but I thought he was excited to speak to me again.

When I did get an opportunity to speak with him, he mentioned he was interested in going out with me and I agreed to it. We got together a few days later. We went out to have a bite to eat and we had more conversations about work and a lot about my son. He asked me if he could meet my son. I was very particular, and I never brought anyone around my son until I got to know what angle a person was coming from. Back in those days, even in these days you just shouldn't bring people around your children without getting to know a person. I told him to give that some time.

After the date, I told him I had a great time and he reached over and kissed my hand. I told him I would talk with him tomorrow and I went home. It almost seemed like he followed me or was timing me or something because as soon as I arrived home he called.

I thought, *"Damn his timing was perfect."*

It seemed flattering but he knew it was late and we both worked early hours. He wanted to chat, however.

After the first date, we connected for dinner after work a few times. I agreed to these short dates because I didn't have childcare for long periods on those days. The next real date we planned for me to spend the night at his house for the weekend. I made plans for my son to go to his grandma's house.

When the weekend came, I packed a bag, and I went to his home. He lived in a back house. We had dinner, watched movies, worked out, and then the sex came. It was cool. We cooked a lot and watched movies the entire weekend. When it was time for me to go, he acted like he didn't want me to. He stated at one point during my visit that he was not letting me go. I told him I had to leave, and I went home.

Over the next few days, we talked, and I noticed he was calling constantly. I had to tell him I was at work, and I would call him back.

One evening, I called him after work once I was settled in to say hello. He had a little bit of an attitude but along with the attitude he sounded very aggressive. He asked why I couldn't talk when he called. I got defensive but I brought it down to respond.

I tried to ease his mind and said, "Hey, I want you to understand during the hours that I am at work I am unable to hold long conversations. I enjoyed the time that I spent with you, and I look forward to seeing you again."

I felt like I shouldn't have had to go there with him, but I did. At this time, we had been seeing each other for a few months.

We got together again. This time I brought him into my house. My son was at my mother's home, and I was comfortable with bringing him to my house because I knew there would not be any interaction between him and my son.

We made love again and it was amazing, but he seemed a bit aggressive again. He started telling me that I had better not see anyone else. I just looked at him because in my opinion it didn't feel like we should be having that conversation.

He grabbed me and pulled me into him and said, "You better not be cheating."

I thought it was cute, not knowing this was only going to get worse.

When we got together, it was predictable. We went out, I went to his house, he came to mine, and this went on for some time. One day, he called me, and I advised him I was not available to see him because I was preparing for training with my job. I would be leaving for a few days and my employer did not give me any notice because the person that was supposed to be going got sick. They needed someone to attend promptly.

He started raising his voice saying that I was lying. I told him I had no need to lie and that I would call him when I got to the location. This guy called me every hour on the hour resulting in my boss becoming furious with me.

When I returned, I went home, and this man was in my home. He didn't have a key. This man got through the bars on my window. He was cooking in my kitchen. I would always leave my windows slightly ajar for ventilation. I was so furious.

He grabbed me by my neck and told me he would

beat the man I was with. I managed to get his hand from around me. I told him not to ever touch me and I explained to him that this training was for work I was so afraid my heart was pounding so fast.

That night he stayed at my house until the next day. He gave the impression he didn't want to go home. I just let him stay. I felt like if I asked him to go it would be an argument. I was fearful.

I went to work that morning, and unfortunately, I had scratches on my neck from him grabbing me. I knew that I had a lunatic on my hands ,but I was afraid to break it off. I thought that convincing him that it was just work would change him, but it would only get worse.

Despite me telling him not to call me at work and that I would call him on a break, he still called. I was going to take my phone off but because I had a child I never wanted to take the phone off, so I silenced the ringer instead. I think my boss was so frustrated with the calls that he fired me. He said the termination was due to budget cuts, but I know that wasn't the case.

After I got fired, the very next day I was out looking for work. I had a lot of responsibility and I had to provide for my son. I was disappointed in myself because I remained with him even after I saw the aggression and the violent behavior.

Finally, in the fifth month of being involved, he and my son connected. Looking at my son's face, I knew he sensed something.

When my son and I were alone, he said, "I don't like him."

The next morning, I got up to go look for work again. He was still at my house, and he said he had taken vacation days. I believe he was lying. I left him there just to keep the bullshit down.

I told him I was going to look for work. I dropped my son off at school. My mom lived in the neighborhood and as I was driving I saw a friend out there watering her grass. I got out of the car, and we were chatting. I looked up and there he was.

He got out of his car, socked me in my face, and shouted, "You lied!"

He jumped back in his car. My friend called 911. I felt prompted to go to the actual police station. I went and I filed a police report. I was scared to leave there.

I filed a restraining order a few days later. This man continued to follow me every day. I got tired of calling the police. I was overwhelmed and exhausted.

The police finally arrested him because he showed up at my house. I didn't press charges because I was afraid. My stupidity. The officers told me he had a record, however, and he would remain in jail. He was in jail for only a few weeks. He attempted to contact me once or twice. I saw his number under my blocked numbers. I was still holding a lot of fear, looking over my shoulder constantly.

I took measures to learn how to protect myself. I took self-defense classes, I got a taser and some pepper spray. I couldn't carry a gun, so I didn't play with the thought. I did not want to get in trouble.

After a few months, things were quiet. I started to feel a little better. Three months later however I had a woman call me and question me about him. She said she had been with him for two years. My mouth fell to the floor. She said he had been beating her, but she loved him, and she was not leaving him. All I could say was wow.

I didn't even go into the whole ordeal about me

and him in detail, but I did tell her we were involved, and it was over. I told her I wished her well, not to worry about me, and that I was sorry because I knew nothing about her.

Finally, this thing was over. I began to feel normal again. Through a mutual friend, I heard that he was working again and with the same woman still beating on her. Unfortunately, moving forward was hard for me. I did not trust people. I was very guarded. I did get counseling. One thing I was grateful for was he didn't have much interaction with my son.

"Until you let go of all the toxic people in your life, you will never be able to grow to your fullest potential. Let them go so you can grow."

Journey 7

When Logic Kicked in

"Before you paint a picture of someone, make sure you don't use your dirty brushes and leave specs on their portrait."

Have you ever been in a relationship that was the best and the worst? Have you ever loved a broken man or woman and just wanted to fix them? At first, in their eyes, you could do no wrong, you are perfect! Until their vision changes you. Literally! It was not that you changed, it's their thoughts that created a new you!

Well, follow me (logic) through my journey of the roller coaster ride I went on for love with a Gemini...

Our first encounter was in passing. I was shopping and he was working. Eventually, I saw him again at the same store. We made eye contact and I proceeded to shop.

When finished, I made my purchase and left the store Unbeknownst to me, he followed me outside and approached me from behind.

"Excuse me," the voice said. "My name is Gemini."

I turned around to face this voice; and it was him.

He said, "I couldn't let you get away again, without saying something."

"Is that right," I responded.

"May I have the pleasure of knowing your name?" he asked.

"Logic."

He looked puzzled.

"My name is Logic."

"Thats different, yet intriguing", he replied."

"How may I help you, Mr. Gemini?"

"I'd like to get your number and just maybe you would let me take you out?"

I hesitated and began to give a reason why not but my niece who was with me persuaded me to give in. I gave him my number and told him to have a good evening.

He smiled and said, "Well, you made my day, so I will have a wonderful evening and walked away.

He called a few times and we talked for several weeks. Then, we planned a date. I met him at the restaurant, so if things went left, I could go right.

The date went very well. As time went on, months passed, we really clicked and enjoyed each other's company. We had great conversations, laughs, and much quality time. Everything was going well. This man moved me in every way. He was a real treat. And I know I was a feast for him!

One day, I told him that me & my kids were going to visit a girlfriend who lived in Moreno Valley, California.

He said, "Cool, give me a call later."

Well, it ended up being a long day of activities. Me & the kids fell asleep and stayed overnight at my girlfriend's. I woke up about 1:30 a.m. looked at my phone and realized I missed his call. So that he wouldn't be concerned, I texted him to let him know I fell asleep, was too tired to drive home, and would head home around 9 a.m.

I messaged him again later that morning to let him know that we were leaving my girlfriend's. No reply. I called, no answer.

When I spoke with him, he had an attitude, and I asked what was up.

He said, "Only thing that happens at 1:30 a.m. in the morning is a booty call."

In disbelief, I questioned his assumption. We went back & forth.

I looked at the phone, said "Later," and ended the conversation.

I had a *'is he serious moment.'* Then, I let it go.

A few days went by, and I received a call as though nothing ever happened. Hhhhmmm. I didn't want to make anything out of it.

Time went on and everything fell back on track. We did everything and had lots of fun along the way. Things couldn't be better. There weren't limitations to where we would go nor what we would do. Parties, picnics, family gatherings, camping, off road riding, dinner, sunset watching, beach walks, Vegas, Laughlin, local casinos and best of all, just sitting and talking.

As we got closer, I noticed changes in his demeanor from time to time. And that was usually when we were in public around people. He was jealous and trusted no man around me. He tended to formulate a theory and act upon it as though it were real. He would trip out on situations, and I didn't understand what the problem was. He would just shut down and not tell me what the issue was. He would cancel plans, not call, or respond to text. This was awkward for me. When he did decide to tell me, the reason was unbelievable. I found myself defending myself on things he conjured up in his head.

One day things would be wonderful and two days, five days, ten days, or one month later there was an issue. He would never state the issue. I guess he assumed that I could read his mind.

He would give the silent treatment. No call, no response to my call or text. Then, when he did come around, he would express what "his thoughts told him I was doing." As time went forward, the accusations became worse and worse. He reacted to what he believed; and when I tried to explain, he would basically say, "any excuse will do, you think I'm deaf, dumb & blind." Whatever the hell that meant.

Why did I need an excuse for things in his head that he could not or did not care to validate? It did not matter if I had proof of my actions. He basically said, "your people will lie for you; you have them all fooled." Huh!!

Debating made absolutely no sense because once it was in his head, he believed it! I went out of my way to prove that his accusations were false. Didn't matter. I was now a liar, a cheater, deceitful and anything else you can think of.

At first, I thought he was playing around. But as these accusations grew deeper and deeper, and happened more frequent, I realized that it was no joke. I had to take a moment to understand exactly what was going on. I tried everything in my power to make him feel secure; and just when I'd think things were better, boom, some more thoughts popped into his head, and we were back on the roller coaster.

I have never had anyone literally conjure up a situation in his head of what I was doing, when he was not around, and believe the thoughts. No matter how many times I tried to remind him of my values, morals, and how good I've been to him, he acted oblivious. He only stuck to the fabricated stories, in his head. It was so demeaning. In his thoughts, I was sexing every man I knew. The theories became deep to where people were telling him that they saw me out with other men. He saw people driving by my house looking for me. Mind you, I lived in a gated community. So, I don't know how he figured the person was looking for me. Oh, because " the driver was a black male."

Basically, every man wanted Logic! And Logic wanted every man. In his eyes. If I didn't call or text him "Goodnight," I was with a man. If I didn't answer his call, I was with a man. But, if he did the same thing, it was no problem, and I was the one trippin. Go figure!

This went on for years. I never knew what I would be accused of next. His thoughts had no boundaries, and I was capable of everything. I got so caught up in defending and proving my innocence, that I lost track of me! So worried about him and doing everything I could to make him feel secure. Living in a world where he was always right; and I could never be.

He would pop up at my home, expecting to find someone with me.

And when he found no one, he said, "They must have left," or "you're just slick."

Everywhere we went, it was always something if

men were close to me. In a casino, playing a table game, I was standing "too close" to the man next to me. Heaven forbid the man asked me a question. Lawd!! While at work, talking to him on the phone, a male co-worker asked me a question and I answered. That was a problem, too.

Spending the day with him and going to the restroom was a problem. One time, he said I took too long and must have been on the phone talking to a man. How was that when I left my phone in his car to charge? I was accused of all kinds of unthinkable shit. And the worst part is that I dealt with all the accusations because I "loved him."

He became verbally disrespectful, using name calling. To him, I was a trifling whore who sucked and f****d, both men & women. It began to literally drive me crazy. I knew I had never done any of the things he accused me of. I think it was more mental for me because I kept trying to use my *logic* on an illogical man.

My name was Logic for a reason. With this man, I lost me in trying to fix him. What was making me stay? Why was I allowing things that I have never allowed before? Why was I defending myself? Why was I allowing this man to manipulate me mentally? Why was I letting this man disrespect me? Why was I so obsessed with fixing him? Why was I not using my name and given talent?

The "logic" in me was gone. He had won by making me an emotional wreck! He succeeded and he knew it, from my actions. I was dancing to his beat. It was no longer about me. It was now all about him.

Usually, I don't consider or include anyone's opinion in my life, however I had to run all this through someone's ear, to give honest feedback. I didn't need agreement, a pity party, just honesty. So, I called my girl, and I shared every uncut, unedited episode. She was speechless and had no idea what I was going through because I never spoke a bad word about Gemini to her. And I was always in a good mood because that's who I am. No one would ever know something was wrong unless I told them.

On our last outing, this man (Gemini) sat in my face and acted like he had no knowledge of the plans we discussed. He went into this long song and dance about how I don't care about him or his health, how I don't do this and didn't do that. Everything was my fault, and he seriously believed what he was saying.

I calmly asked, "What can I do to make this day right so we can enjoy the rest of this day?"

He continued rambling, without answering, then said, "What's the point if this is how our day is going!"

Then the word, "BITCH," flew out his mouth.

I made that exorcist turn, "Did you just call me a "BITCH, your sorry SOB!!"

"Yeah," he replied.

It took everything in me not to slap the shit out of him. Right then was the last straw for me.

"Logic" kicked in. I strapped up (my seatbelt), started the car, and began to drive. He kept talking shit and I just drove because if I responded to him, it wasn't gonna end well. He was no longer worth my time or energy.

I drove to my house where his car was parked. I got out, left him sitting there, and went inside my house. A few minutes later, there was a knock at my door. I opened the door and there his stupid ass stood.

"Can we talk?" he asked.

"About what?!" I replied?

I let him in. We stared at one another for a moment, in silence.

"What now?" he said.

I laughed!

Then, he had the audacity to say, "So are you gonna get naked?"

I politely stood up, walked to him, placed my voluptuous thighs between his legs, leaned forward, and gave him a long, slow, exotic kiss, to his arousal. I moved back, grabbed his hands; he stood up. I turned to walk, as if the intent was to oblige his request.

As I approached the door, I turned for what I knew would be his last kiss. Then, I opened the door, turned to face him, and really said "BOY BYE!"

I was so proud of myself! I loved him, but I loved me more. I was done with his toxic roller coaster that took me on loops, dips, and many curves. The spell was broken. I freed myself of the bondage and power that I allowed to control me.

I am a realist. He could not have done anything had I not allowed it. I pray for him and all the women he pursues. The next ride ain't on me! Heaven help them!

You might assume that I had low self-esteem. But that was not it. I was in love and for me this was the best & the worse relationship ever. That's what made it hard for me. I am a fixer and after years of trying I finally realized that Gemini was broken long before me, and he will be broken long after me. I am faithful and I believe people can change. I believe he thinks he is God, perfect, and everyone else is and will always be the problem. He was beyond my ability and bottom line, love was finally defeated when Logic, kicked in. AS SHE ALWAYS DOES.

I Am "LOGIC."
L-isten
O-bserve
G-ather
I-nvestigate
C-onclude

I DO, I DID, I'm DONE!

"The wrong person will give you less than what you're worth but that doesn't mean that you have to accept it."

Journey 8

Untitled

I should've ran when I saw this man had nothing but issues. I was very empathic because I had my own issues and I had known him since I was a teenager. We never dated in our younger years. I met him when I had just turned seventeen years old. Our relationship when we were younger was just best friends. I was even close to his mom. I used to go to church with them. My mom and stepdad started going back to church with us because I was going and trying to become better, and they wanted to as well. Our families became super close because of this.

I had originally met him through my first boyfriend, they used to be friends at one point, and we all used to be roommates. We remained friends throughout the years. I never saw any red flags in the nine years we had been friends already. He was always so good to me and my family, and so was his mom. He even used to do my mom's yard work to help her out.

When we were younger, he did want to be with me, but I was never ready for the things he wanted such as marriage or starting a family. I always encouraged us to remain friends and for him to seek someone who was a better fit for what he currently wanted out of life. I was not in the same place at the time and knew I wouldn't be anytime soon. Eventually, he took to this advice and moved on.

He got married and started a family. I was genuinely happy for him because I knew he always wanted that. I even tried to extend my hand to her to be friends as well. Even though we really tried to be friends and had some good times together, she didn't ever fully trust me not to have ulterior motives and it made me pull away. It got uncomfortable for me simply because I respected their marriage and was hoping for the best and I'm not the type to force any friendships.

Throughout the years, however, he and I would still casually check on each other, wishing well onto each other. Everything was still platonic between us during their marriage because I am a woman's woman at the end of the day, and I always have been like that. When their marriage ended, meaning she left him and moved on, he started consistently pursuing me.

At that point, I had a daughter and the situation with her dad hadn't worked so I was open to having something more with him. By then we seemed to have values that aligned with each other, and I was ready to be a part of a family because I've always been denied by the one I was born into. And again, he and his family were always good to me, so he seemed safe to me at the time.

We started dating, then moved in together. At first, everything was amazing. He was really caring and helpful with certain things and we were working well as a team. Everything seemed perfect. Until they weren't.

I started noticing red flags when the smallest of boundaries weren't being respected. I'm neurodivergent and I have issues with sensory overload. Sometimes it triggers such massive anxiety it can make me irritated, lightheaded, give me painful headaches and so on. And although I expect no one to have to walk on eggshells because of me, I do expect to be respected when I ask for space in a different room to avoid whatever is triggering me. I never felt that was asking for much. But it would cause massive arguments and he'd go to his mom's house for a day or two. Later, I found out it was so I could be cheated on with his ex-wife but that would only be revealed to me later.

One day, he started bringing up having a baby. I always insisted I'd like to wait until things are better financially for us and our romantic relationship has some longevity behind it as well because I do not want to end up being a single mom of two. He acted as if he understood where I was at and would leave it alone and casually bring it up here and there in different ways. I didn't realize he was already planning to get me pregnant right away and I should have taken more heed to what he was saying. I just thought he was optimistic about us having a future and was willing to wait.

As fate would have it, I found out I was pregnant. I was shocked because I didn't think this would happen. Even though I do not take birth control, I'm really good about tracking my cycles and not getting pregnant. It worked for five years. I realized it had to have happened that one night I was under the influence.

As soon as I got pregnant, he became a whole

different person and he turned into a different type of evil. I believe he thought I wouldn't be able to leave him because now I'd have two kids and he knew I didn't want to be a single mom again. This is when I realized he's a narcissist and I needed to make an exit plan.

Unfortunately, I had been let go from a job right before finding out about my pregnancy. Financially, I didn't have a lot of options. I was down to my last dimes.

During pregnancy testing, I was told I had a sexually transmitted infection (STI). I confronted him about it. He admitted to sleeping with his ex-wife without protection when we had gotten into a disagreement.

He started making it impossible for me to seek new employment by leaving his kids with me instead of taking them to daycare. What was I supposed to do? Leave his two toddlers there by themselves, especially when they were craving love and attention desperately. I tried to give them everything they were lacking. Their dad ignored them, and their mom was in active addiction putting herself and her kids in harm's way every time they were with her. It was so bad that his son came home with a black eye one day. My heart hurt and cried for the kids so bad.

Asking family and friends for help was not an option for me. I didn't have a supportive system. In fact, it was very broken and somewhat still is. So, I had to be strategic and smart about it. I walked on eggshells. I pretended everything was okay and I pretended to be grateful he was working so hard to provide. I cleaned, I took care of his kids, I cooked all the meals and even made sure he had lunch to take to work.

That's when it went from emotional abuse to physical abuse. His method of physical abuse is strangulation - to the point of passing out or almost passing out. This is very important. Statistically strangulation is often a predictor of a future homicide. Strangulation alone increases your chances of being a victim of homicide by 750%. I was very aware of this. The clock was ticking for me to make a move towards safety. I had no time to play games. I just wanted to survive this and not get an eviction. Everything was in my name, which added so much sensitivity to the situation while simultaneously handing more power over to him. If I ever got an eviction, I knew me, and my kids would never be able to find somewhere to live again. At least for a long time in my state. And my state is drastically lacking resources currently.

I had a plan. I started pressuring his mom to agree to watch the kids more because I'm "really sick from pregnancy" and I "needed a break sometimes." She barely did it. But as soon as they were with her, or they went to their moms I was Door Dashing and putting money away he didn't know about. I was hoping there wouldn't be another attack and I could execute my plan seamlessly, but it didn't work like that.

We got into an argument because he was throwing trash everywhere on the ground. Food wrappers, blunt wrappers, you name it. I felt very disrespected because I had been cleaning, taking care of his kids, and picking up after them all day and I owned multiple trash cans. Me expressing my frustration pissed him off. He started saying I should be grateful that he works to provide. But I couldn't even pretend anymore, I was miserable.

He started packing all of his and his kids' stuff. He was so mad he wasn't paying attention to what he was picking up and picked up my stuff and my daughter's stuff into his bags. He grabbed a blanket I had since I was a child that was my daughter's current favorite thing to sleep with the days she was at my house.

So, I said, "That's mine," and I reached for it.

Next thing I knew, I was being choke slammed into the hard corner of my bed. He started strangling me again and beating my head into it. He took my car keys and my apartment keys and left.

Something didn't feel right. I was very lightheaded, disoriented, and nauseated. And this attack was a lot worse. I called him and begged him to bring me back my keys so I could go to the hospital, and he kept hanging up on me or sending me to voicemail. Now I had to call emergency services because I needed to make sure my baby was okay.

When the ambulance showed up, the police did as well. The officer noticed my bruises and the state of my apartment. He knew it was domestic violence related. He took it very personally because I used to serve him at the bar I worked at, and he knew me already through that. He threatened to arrest me if I didn't comply and tell him who did it. And I refused to go to jail because of something someone else did to me. I did what I had to do, which was tell the truth.

They found him and he got arrested for battery on a woman who is pregnant. When he got bonded out by his mother, the order stated there was to be no contact made with me. It was perfect because now I had the documentation needed so I could break my lease without an eviction because domestic violence victims have rights that protect them as tenants in my state.

I made arrangements to make it to a domestic shelter. I packed up what I could fit in my Nissan Versa and never looked back. I'm still at the shelter. I've since had my son.

I work very hard to provide. I wish I could say things are amazing now. But It's very emotionally and financially draining. Especially since I'm still trying to pay off debt that his dad has caused me. But the love I have for my son is incredible and I can sleep in peace at night knowing me and my kids are safe from harm's way. That is a huge blessing.

I think sometimes you don't even realize how much safety means until you're faced with certain situations. One thing I've learned by working in behavioral health with pediatric patients is that kids learn a lot by what you do and not by what you say. I'm glad I showed my daughter she should never accept that behavior from a man and I'm glad my son is not going to grow up thinking I'd even allow him to put his hands on a female. Your daughters will be safe with him due to my decisions. I don't care how hard things are, and I don't care how hard they look right now because times are still incredibly uncertain for me. But I can always stand on my decision to leave this man. I'm the definition of a momma who's going to make it happen. Nobody can take that away from me. And I'll keep fighting for my happy ending.

"The most painful thing is losing yourself in the process of loving someone too much and forgetting that you are special too."

Journey 9

Right Man + Wrong Time=A Hot Mess from Hell

Dear Lord God,

I need your presence and guidance in presenting me to a Godly man to become my husband. I ask for Your grace to lead me to a man of integrity, who is not only devoted to you, but also seeks to live out your teachings in his daily life. May he be a man passionate for the things of God and we both work in ministry together with zeal building the Kingdom of God. May he be a leader who walks in faith, integrity, and reverence in your sanctuary.

I pray for a partner who walks with you and prays with me, but also understands the depths of my heart. Someone who, through their own life experiences, comprehends the struggles and challenges that come with a difficult past. I envision finding solace and understanding, knowing that he, too, has faced adversity and emerged with a compassionate heart, ready to embrace and support others in their healing journey.

I'm seeking someone to grow old together with.

Someone who'd also be my best friend. May I be aligned to your will and may this be led by Your Holy Spirit. May this be a divine meeting and in Your will in Jesus' name I pray, Amen.

My first marriage had failed. I had dated unsuccessfully, and I wanted to try love again. I asked God to pick the person that's right for me.

I was working at the beauty counter in a department store at the Fox Hills Mall when I first met Lovell's cousin. Sharkesha was looking for makeup when she struck up a conversation. It was an amicable exchange. She wanted my number to keep in touch and invited me to visit her church.

Happily, I went. It was dissimilar from most churches I attended in the past. I went to churches where the people were reserved, with the occasional outbreak of shouting. When I visited the church, people, and the pastor, I was ecstatic over the worship and praise there. I enjoyed the fact that they were radical with their praise and the pastor I felt had a depth that I could relate to in the message he was preaching. Sharkesha introduced me to the pastor, and I started attending more often.

Sharkesha told me that her cousin and I would be perfect for each other. She could see our future. She was already playing the matchmaker. She felt he kept running into the wrong women and because I had a job and showed some type of responsibility, I might be good for him. I was somewhat curious; we were introduced over the phone. The conversation was great, he sounded like a nice guy.

The next Sunday, I went to visit again and that's when she introduced us. I wasn't attracted to him at all. His voice didn't match his face or at least how I imagined he would look. He looked like he came from a foreign country - Africa. I couldn't see us together at all and so I said no.

He said he felt something, like there was a connection in our conversation over the phone. I just couldn't see it and I said no. That didn't stop him. He expressed interest in getting to know me better.

Life intervened as I found myself relocating out of town for a year. I packed my belongings and set off on new interests and self-discovery. My aspirations were the ambitious plan to establish my own fashion company in the picturesque landscapes of Georgia. However, reality deviated from my envisioned path, leaving me with unforeseen experiences. Life in a new location proved to be harder than I anticipated. The distances to travel were a stark contrast with the busy hustle of Los Angeles. Yet, with what seemed like limitations to traveling within the state, Georgia had its own unique charms with its vast beauty and the shops felt like a great place to settle in.

Experiencing all four seasons, when it was spring it was perfect weather with blooms of flowers, butterflies, and bees floating. Summer was hot and humid with no escape to breathe. Fall, with the dramatic spectacle of thunderstorms that rumbled echoing rage, came without apologies. But the biting cold of winter, even my sturdiest jackets and coats were inadequate against the icy 17 degrees Fahrenheit. That year was distinct in so many ways, unlike California where it's mostly sunny days.

After a year, I went back home to California to regain footage, in my goals, including other endeavors. Reunited with friends telling them about what I'd seen along with what I've experienced. I soon decided to visit that church in which I liked that the woman invited me to a year prior.

Sharkesha remembered me and we reconnected, also her cousin was not too far behind. I started attending that same church. Finding myself sitting next to Sharkesha and her daughters, I eventually became a member. She invited me to her home. In our conversations, she was still mentioning her cousin and I making a good couple. She and I spent time together becoming better acquainted and it seemed a friendship was blooming.

As time went by, I felt drawn to Lovell. We would have conversations and spend time talking after church. At one point, Sharkesha, Lovell, and I were spending time after church with each other. During our conversations I saw a glimpse of his heart. I started seeing his potential, believed he really loved God, furthermore ministry seemed to be his focus.

The dreamer in me saw a purpose in us coming together. I listened to his words as we were dating. He talked a bit about his life and about not feeling supported by family. In those moments, I felt compassion for what he was going through. I felt he was relatable because there were many times I felt no support coming from my own family.

As the weeks passed on, we walked, went out, talked, and I started feeling closer to him. It was natural and organic, not forced. In a few months, we were engaged.

He met my family at a church where my children were doing mime ministry. I noticed he didn't introduce me to his family right away, so I brought it up. It was strange and bewildering, yet over time I met a few people from his family, then his father.

I noticed he kept saying no one was there for him

or cared about him in his family but I saw otherwise. The very people he kept saying weren't there for him, were in fact there. Perhaps they weren't there in the way he wanted. I also noticed that he believed people were supposed to help him. I saw that people did what they could, yet there were times I saw them doing more than enough. I noticed he had a sense of entitlement when it came to how they helped or what they asked of him. I tried to rationalize with him about what he was expecting and what he was saying. He didn't seem to catch on to the fact that no one owed him anything and that family did not have to help him.

At first, I just took it as his family having disagreements, then I realized he was ungrateful and unthankful. Those were red flags, areas where he needed to grow up. I still supported him emotionally over his experiences while trying to get him to see it from their perspective as well.

We stayed engaged, despite what I realized about him. I still felt that he was the right person for me. I kept feeling and getting spiritual confirmations, where the Holy Spirit was talking to me. I thought about pulling out of the relationship but there were many things that confirmed that God was in it and moving. I prayed, fasted, and questioned was he truly the one.

There were many confirmations and signs that reassured me that I was with the right person. Once, we spoke about having a beach wedding over the phone. I was working on my computer searching for something online. As I was searching, I came across a wedding cake that was so beautiful. It was beach themed with shells, I was amused, it seemed to be a sign.

Another time, no one not even others outside of

our relationship could deny: He was at church as an armorbearer with the pastor of our church and I was talking with my mom. There conversations were happening simultaneously. The pastor told my fiancé at that moment that a nice wedding would be a certain undisclosed amount. I was with my mother talking with her and she said that the Holy Spirit told her that our wedding should be a certain undisclosed amount of dollars.

When Lovell and I both came together to speak about what was said. It blew both of our minds, we were in different parts of the city, and we all had the same conversation without the other knowing. My mother nor the pastor had met each other at that time nor were they in the same room. How could they say the same exact dollar amount of money that the wedding should cost?

Another time we were at his job, and he introduced me to his boss and co-workers saying this is my fiancé.

One of the ladies said, "Hello Mr. Jones, Mrs. Jones."

It made me feel so joyful; it was blissful. I had so many confirmations that I knew things couldn't go wrong.

People started walking up to him telling him that God was going to give him a daughter. One prophet told him that we were going to have a daughter together and that she was going to be a worldwide evangelist. After a year of courting, we married... too soon! I wished we had waited longer. I originally stated two years of courting, we needed to build a stronger foundation to protect our marriage, yet he wanted to marry sooner. I already knew that we were growing in love, but he wanted electric magnetic love.

I felt that I loved him, but it was a calm and steady

growth for me, and I felt our realities on that were different. There was other ground that we needed to cover which we didn't get all in one year. He told me that he had a place, and I made the wrong assumption. Because we were talking about our lives together, I thought he got a place on his own. I thought I would be moving in with my husband alone. Instead, he kept something from me – he was living with a roommate, who happened to be a friend of his.

I felt upset over the deception. I thought someone was in the other room, but he told me that he just had boxes that he hadn't unpacked yet when I attempted to open the door and it was locked. I heard noises but he told me it was the other apartment. But that lie was short lived because I knew those footprints weren't from another apartment like he was trying to make me believe. He finally confessed only because I heard someone in the bathroom flushing the toilet (he must have thought I was a quiet sleeper) I was introduced to his roommate the next day.

I thought it was bizarre and I thought about the plans we made, our wedding plans and our talks about how we were going to set our life up and how we were going to come together. But being in it already I just accepted his mistake, forgave him, and pushed past it... The reality is that I was married, living with my husband and his roommate. It felt like a joke and like I was dealing with boys, but I still loved him.

During our time at that apartment with his roommate, I was embarrassed that this was the start of our life. I didn't tell anyone except a few family members. I loved my husband and wanted to push past this grave deception.

We went on to live our life in that situation. Not too far from the beginning, he started showing signs of insecurities and emotional instability. He would accuse me of cheating, and I was totally confused. Then, he would say that I didn't love him and would turn around the next day and say that I was the best thing that happened in his life.

Our pastor told me that there were three people praying against our marriage, and one person was his cousin, the one that wanted us to be together! I was praying mostly alone during our marriage. Lovell prayed with me sometimes, but he didn't have the same discipline. He seemed to always be angry, and it was out of control.

He would leave his job to check on me to see if I were cheating. I found myself having to reassure him repeatedly that I wouldn't have married him unless I loved him. But he was paranoid, and constantly saying that I didn't love him. It was becoming weighty and heavy on my heart.

You can't war alone in a marriage. I not only prayed but started anointing our house, bed, and praying over the walls of our home. Whatever spirit that was sent to him only seemed to be getting worse. I asked God what was going on as I was praying warfare prayers. God showed me I was killing demons one at a time. I thought the demon rose back up, but God showed me that it was a network of demons working overtime to destroy the marriage. As I was slaying demons, more were coming. It wasn't the same one but different ones coming back-to-back.

Lovell was our pastors armorbearer, but he even pulled away from that because of the attacks that went with ministry. Then he started going to church less. I prayed heavily.

Things didn't seem to let up, I was being accused of cheating to the point my soul was vexed, and I wished he'd stop. No one wants to be falsely accused. He left work when no one was looking, drove the company's vehicle to our place to see if I was home with another man. He wanted to know if I invited a man over while he was at work. It wasn't normal, and I started wondering if he was on drugs or Schizophrenic, with all his bizarre behavior and wild accusations.

Once I was asleep, I suppose he tried texting me, but I was tired. I felt a presence standing over me and it didn't feel right. I woke up, opened my eyes, only to see him lurking over me watching me sleep and I asked him what was wrong and why wasn't he at work. Apparently instead of thinking I might have fallen asleep since it was late at night, if I didn't answer the phone, he thought I was with another man.

It became hell. He would pick fights from out of the blue and it was confusing. He would come home late at night, and I would make sure dinner was ready for him but nothing I did he was grateful for. Some nights we had sex before he went to sleep. Sometimes I fell asleep, he would then wake me up at 2 or 3 a.m. to have sex. I woke up at 6 a.m. daily. I didn't see the problem since I needed a couple more hours of rest. I didn't mind late nights either but the times I was extremely tired, he got demanding and would pick fights lasting for two to three hours, instead of letting me sleep.

His anger would perpetuate when I didn't respond like he wanted me to. He would say that I didn't' love him because I wouldn't yell and participate in the arguments. I would look at him wondering if this man was serious.

Once when I did finally flip out, it was like there was a demon inside of him because he smiled when I started expressing being upset. He nearly drove me crazy. My hair began to fall out, and it was thinning from the stress of dealing with him.

His phone rang one day, and I tried to get him to see how ridiculous he was.

So, I start mimicking him, saying, "Hey is that your girlfriend calling you?"

I picked up his phone because he wasn't saying anything. He just stood still. I gave him the phone and was about to say just joking when he grabbed me saying don't ever touch him again. I didn't touch him, I only handed him the phone and I told him so.

He grabbed my shoulders and slammed my body against the wall, dragging me across the wall from one end to the other as if I were a rag doll. He started fighting me and I wasn't hitting back. I couldn't push him off me and I couldn't get out of his grip. He was about to body slam me on to the floor. I don't know how but I talked him out of doing that and threatened to leave right then and there. I found myself washing off my scraped skin cells, fibers from the dress, and the dye from my dress from our white walls.

After that, I started making plans to get a savings together and start strategizing when to leave. It had been eight months, and I felt like I had made the biggest mistake of my life. I pretended that all was well but was making plans to exit.

I couldn't even go to the corner convenience store to get chips and soda without him thinking I was going to meet someone. I liked to dress nice, so grooming my hair and putting on light makeup was my thing, but he saw it as I wanted someone else.

His roommate lost his job and didn't find another one, so Lavell wanted him out and kicked him out. That brought some drama with his friend/roommate. We ended up leaving the apartment because our income wasn't enough for the 2 bedrooms. We separated, but I was drained by him.

I was working one day at another office, and he was calling me saying mean things and making more false accusations. I was crying so hard and hoping no one would see me. He was twisting truth around and while I was bawling my eyes out and crying hard at work. He called me, texted me, and I tried to explain things to him. I even sent several messages, yet he twisted things around and called me crazy for contacting him, yet he contacted me.

I can't explain it but something inside of me just said stop. I felt a calmness and clarity moment. I didn't have to put up with it! I had enough money saved, we weren't living together, I could close the storage, leave him alone, and divorce him.

I decided I couldn't take it anymore. I packed my bags and left. I wasn't going to keep dealing with the emotional and psychological abuse, the ups and downs that were drastic. The arguments that he would start from out of the blue when there wasn't even a problem. I don't know if he was cheating. It's a possibility after all the accusations. They say that if they accuse, they are doing it themselves. What I knew was love doesn't take away your peace. Love is peaceful.

He told me that he never knew a couple to live in harmony. I think he lived a life so chaotic in his past that he never healed from the trauma he experienced in his life. He brought that into the marriage. I found myself being the one who was understanding and patient with him, but he wasn't giving me anything but nausea. My stomach began to turn at the thought of him and I knew it was over for me. Those were generational curses that he didn't break at that point, and it was destroying us.

He needed healing and I needed healing after the trauma he brought into my life. There was more inner work that needed to be done on both of our sides. He projected his own issues onto me. And I needed to heal what was in me that put up with him as long as I did.

One of my best friends, Jermaine said, "I know you loved him because you never put up with people's mess."

I did love him. But all the hell and chaos he brought into my life was not worth it. I lost myself, I didn't recognize me. It hurt but love wasn't going to keep me back.

I told myself that day, "I love me more than you. I love God more than you." I filed for divorce and moved on. Boy Bye!

"It's amazing how someone can break your heart and you can still love them with all the little pieces."

Journey 10

Eat the Meat, Spit out the Bones
(Devil in Disguise)

He said, "You are my dream girl. You are who I have asked God for all my life. So now I can say that dreams do come true!"

Boy BYE! That was not my response then of course but keep reading and you will see clearly why this is my response now.

"10, 9, 8, 7, 6, 5, 4, 3, 2,1... HAPPY NEW YEAR!!!"

I was locked into the arms of the man I thought God had personally hand selected for my life. He was strong, boy was he strong. He was kind and he was gentle. He was patient and heck he was willing to put up with my mess. Lord knows I have some and he looked past it all, allowing me to be open, transparent, and free to share my deepest thoughts.

He allowed me to be me: a vibrant extrovert, full of life, energy, and passionate about Christ. He was just the opposite: an introvert, quiet, reserved, and very particular of who he lets in and what he lets out. But he didn't miss a beat when it came to me. He did not play about me, he loved me and was not shy about it. He was HUGE on PDA. For those of you who don't know what PDA is, no worries, I just found out, too - it's public display of affection.

It was amazing how he loved me. I felt like a teenager again. I wanted for NOTHING. He met EVERY need, mentally, physically, emotionally, and financially. It was not an easy win for him though.

I had known him for 9.5 years by the time I finally let him in. We played around with the idea very early on, but life happened, and it was just a NO! However, he was there, through new loves, heart break, and even a baby after my son's father passed suddenly. He prayed with me, he comforted me, and he waited for me.

My heart was guarded. He helped me dodge the bullet of someone we both knew, me better than him. But he had given me the inside scoop on how a man thinks - one of MANY red flags that I ignored early on. He stuck close, being there for the children, and helping me to cope through possible issues later down the line. Who was this man? He was my angel, so I thought. But this angel broke my heart.

"Are you married or attached to anyone?" I asked.

He answered, "No, baby."

"Is there anyone that is attached to you?" I probed.

He answered, "No baby, I have been single for the past 10 years, just working and staying busy. I knew deep down you were it for me. If I could not have you, I didn't want anyone. I dated but my heart was with you, you are my dream girl. I let you get away before, but I promised God if I got another chance I would not mess it up."

I melted because I too had been praying for God to

send my King because who wants to be alone?! And hell, if you fall off of your bike 30 times, does that mean you don't get back on it again? No, it just means you learn from your mistakes, so you don't fall again, at least not in the same places right? Whelp, that's what I thought I was doing.

I had strapped on my shoelaces. I had taken that time to self-reflect, emptied out all the previous experiences on those past bike rides and y'all I ate the meat and I spit out the bones. Unfortunately, there is always one that disguises itself so well within the meat that you don't realize it is a bone and you swallow it. At least you try to, but it gets stuck there and you need something stronger to help get it down like water and a piece of bread. In this case, for me, that bone was this angel, though he should have been one of those thrown out, he stuck around disguised as someone to keep.

There were many red flags, but the help I sought after was the blood of Jesus, the living water and His flesh to help me cope through them. Besides, He is the one that sent him right?! It clearly had to be me with residue from my past and I should not make him pay for something he had not done, right?! Boy BYE!

I had so many signs and reasons to walk away, but I could not. This was my angel; he had looked past all my flaws, why couldn't I look past his? So, I did. Once I questioned him about something that didn't sit right in my spirit, and he gave me such an amazing response. I was like, *"Girl, don't you push him away. It's you, not him."* I would find myself not responding to what I saw were problems hell because everything was a problem for me. So, I had to humble myself and give him a little wiggle room. I needed to give him time to adjust to being in a relationship, again.

I was a serial-situationshiper. (I just made that up, feel free to use it.) He doesn't have small children, so I forced myself to be patient with him as he had been with me. I had talked to myself and prayed myself out of walking out of the door on multiple occasions. *"You have always been the one to leave, do something different if you want something different,"* is what I kept telling myself.

I became less opinionated and less vocal and even more of a prayer warrior, not against him but for him. This was something I had not learned to do previously. It was working. He was quick to apologize, we didn't argue nor raise our voices to each other.

He was always calm and would say, "Baby, I love you. I won't hurt you."

He would take me shopping, send me cash, or ship me something - flowers, chocolates, something for the kids, always SOMETHING. This would melt my heart and he knew it. It became our thing and I loved how he loved me. Again, I wanted for NOTHING and he paid for EVERYTHING. My son became his son. One time, he even threatened to take me to court when I didn't want to talk to him anymore as friends.

He said, "You can stop talking to me, but don't take my son from me."

It was just amazing to have a man to fight for me as well as a child of mine that he had no pleasure in making.

With all of that, something was just not right in my spirit about him. We traveled together, he stayed over at my place, he was in. He was in, he was "MY MANNN!"

He remained consistent and it was three months of joy. A 9-year friendship had turned into a lifetime love story. No, literally!

We took a road trip for 10 days, just he and I. Just the two of us. We had nothing to do but talk, eat, and explore all of the east coast (and some of the west coast). It was one of the things on my bucket list. During this 10 days, it was a fairytale. He was so attentive. We prayed, had bible study, went to church service, the usual. We enjoyed dinner and wine, shopping, and all of the normal things we enjoyed doing together.

It was strange to me that his phone never rang.

In previous conversations, I had asked, "Where are your friends?"

Always having an amazing response because he was quick on his feet, he'd say, "I have them, just don't talk often."

"What about your family? I mean, no one calls you," I'd probe.

His response was, "Because I am boring and into God now, so I lost a lot of connections because of my changed lifestyle."

It was the same response all of the time and each time I bought what he was selling. Until he was putting the TV together in the truck. I happened to look back and saw "Jason Spencer" as his Wi-Fi.

I saw that name before and asked, "Who is Jason Spencer?"

He responded, "Oh shoot, I selected the wrong one."

My eyebrow raised. I turned away to look at my phone as he searched for the "correct" Wi-Fi.

The Holy Spirit said, "Look."

Wouldn'y you know Jason Spencer happened to pop up again. Well, you know my "angel," always quick on his feet gave some very sellable answer, only this time I wasn't buying it. My angel was shook!

"Who is Jason Spencer?"

What I had not picked up on is these were his same initials. But what I did pick up on is that he had emailed me 10 years ago from a similar email address. While he was explaining yet again that it was someone else's Wi-Fi, he just happened to keep selecting it and even putting in a password, I was researching. I went to my email and searched Jason Spencer. Bingo! This *Jason* had emailed me. The most recent time was in 2019 asking me had my son, our son, arrived. I had not paid any attention to the "Jason'" thing as 2019 was a beast in itself. So, an email address was the least of my concerns. But it was a huge concern in this season.

He fought me tooth and nail trying to convince me that he had never seen that Wi-Fi before.

I said to him, as I was looking at this email on my phone, "Baby, I love you, please be honest."

Again, he swore to his innocence.

I became quiet, as I prayed. I felt the old me rising up. We were in the middle of nowhere and this man was trying to convince me that it is the Wi-Fi for someone else. It made no sense, and he had no reason to lie. Yet I began to doubt myself.

He had just purchased the TV and the phone, so maybe?....GIRL BYE!! I snapped out of that, and I reminded him that he had emailed me with that name 10 years ago. I also reminded him of what he told me, still not letting him know I was looking right at the emails. He parted his lips to look me straight in the eyes saying how he never told me that he was signed into someone else's account by mistake at the fire department. So convincing, I almost second guessed what was staring me dead in my eyes on my screen.

He lied so well. His voice would drop, his speech would slow, and his words became so soothing. Telling me he never told me that, he tried to continue, even trying to change the subject. Because like before, he was so good at doing so, it just had to work this time, too.

Then, he reminded me that we needed to go shopping for the things we missed on our many other trips to shop during that week.

I quickly interrupted, "Before you lie AGAIN, know that I am looking right at the email! You CLEARLY stated that it was someone else's account and not once but twice, you used it by mistake. So, please think before you speak."

Still not looking at him, because I was going to SNAP if he lied again, this fool proceeded to tell me, "Okay, I lied."

I wanted to say no SUGAR, but I wanted to use the other "S" word. Instead, I let him speak. That now soothing voice just screams, "BRACE YOURSELF, I'M ABOUT TO LIE," and that's exactly what he did.

I looked at him crazy and asked, "Are you kidding me? Is that the best you can come up with?"

He responded, "Well, yes, because it is the truth. I'm sorry baby and I understand if you don't believe me because I let a 10-year-old lie hurt us, but it is the truth." He continued, "That's why it's not good to lie because you have to tell another to cover the first lie. But it was before us, and I should have been deleted it from my phone."

Prior to that, what seemed to be an amazing confession, I had also checked to see if that Wi-Fi would be available for my phone. It was there, clear, and ready for a password. Now, part of his such wonderful explanation, he never created the Wi-Fi, had never used it, and just so happened to pop up with the phone, but he was going to change the email address, so it won't pop up again. Whelp, while he was speaking, that Wi-Fi option was no longer an option for me.

I asked, "So are you going to delete the email so that particular Wi-Fi address won't show up again? Because you didn't create it, it was only attached to that email, right?"

He said, "Correct."

I told him that I didn't believe him, but I would let it go. Still thinking I can only see the Wi-Fi from the TV, he proceeded to delete the email. Can I tell you later that night "Jason Spencer" popped back up.

I was disappointed. I knew he was still lying to me, and I told him so. I pleaded with him during that now drawn-out vacation to be honest with me. I told him that I needed to be let in; He promised that was it and he expressed how terrible he felt about letting me down. He said he would never again do so.

This still did not sit well with me. RED FLAGS were going up all over. There were so many incidents that I had looked past because he was so convincing, but God would not let me let this go.

I continued to ask about our future, and explained to him the importance more now than ever of letting me in. I expressed this to him previously during a cruise while shopping for wedding rings, which he initiated, only to be disappointed because his credit was not in place to get it at the time, but I understood. He preferred to pay cash for the ring and promised we would be back for it. He planned for us to fly back for the ring from the U.S. in the upcoming month.

When that time came, well you know something came up. But I dismissed it. I was not going to let me talk myself out of this amazing man.

Back to this road trip, which was actually three months since my birthday cruise that we took together. We had searched for ring after ring since he wanted me as his wife. However, he didn't want to get married if we didn't have the ring I wanted from the Bahamas. It was a beautiful ring, so yes that worked before. But I reminded him that this was not about a ring, it was about God. He agreed and suggested that he and God had been talking and he already knew the next step.

"You do? So, God gave you a date?" I inquired.

He said, "Yup, so I need you to let me and God do what we do."

I smiled and said, "OKAY!"

I mean, he did say God told him and all, so it must be true!

So, the rest of that day we were on cloud 9. We were booed up, loved up, and so excited about US. We went shopping, put some clothes on and went out on the town. He did it big that night as we do anytime he took me out. But this time, it was even better. He knew he was back in my good grace and wanted to celebrate the win.

The next morning, we were just a couple days before making it home from this 10-day road trip. We got ready for the day and went to a nice breakfast. I had a dream the night before. God was trying to tell me something, I just didn't know what. I shared it with him.

In short, the dream consisted of us being in a car. I was the driver and he the passenger. Suddenly, a bike rider came and hit the car on the passenger side where he sat. I can recall in the dream noticing we were about to hit fly. I grabbed the steering wheel with one hand to control it so the impact wouldn't be so dreadful, however it still was.

I flew out of the car and was hurt pretty bad, and he was nowhere to be found. I remember in the dream seeing my body on the ground. My eyes were moving, and I could see I was breathing but clearly I was unconscious.

I recall the medic asking, "Has she ever been awake?"

I responded, "YES," before waking up.

He didn't know what to make out of the dream and dismissed it. But I was uneasy and believe that God was speaking.

After prayer, I received my answer. It was confirmed by a good sister in Christ. I was no longer awake; I was losing control of my inner voice. I was so busy trying to save *us* that I was losing me. If I continued to deny the voice within (Holy Spirit) it was going to kill me because I was being disobedient. Immediately, I repented. I asked God for guidance in this. I pleaded for Him to speak louder than ever before and that's what He did. It's what He had been doing, I simply needed to listen and shut out the other voices.

Later that week, I noticed a tattoo on him that I had been seeing for years, but suddenly it stood out. That night, I was prompted to ask his daughter's name again. He confirmed the name that was tatted on his arm. I knew he was lying, immediately. I just knew! This was the first time in 10 years that I questioned it, but it was a vital piece of this puzzle.

The next morning, I went to him again, "Baby, I love you. You have loved me and my children, but you keep me at a distance from your world, why? What are you hiding?"

Once again, he declared his innocence, how he wants us to get married soon, and next month we will go see his family. Then, he insisted that we go to one of my favorite breakfast spots, Iron Rooster. Before that, we went shopping for me and our son. This was nice, but at this point, I was uncomfortable. I couldn't confirm it, but my inner voice was not resting on this name story. I began to follow the breadcrumbs. I told myself that until this was settled, we would not go on another trip, and he was not welcomed in my home again.

I was UNCOMFORTABLE with my friend of 9.5 years turned LOVE. What was going on? Holy Spirit spoke and continued to speak. I continued to listen as well as acted on that of what was being said instead of dismissing the clues.

***

Now I had concrete evidence.

I called him and I pleaded with him, "Please, my love, let me in, I need you to be honest, we are all flawed, just be honest with me. Who is Janetta?"

He responded, "My ex."

For a second, I began to question the facts that I had. But that inner voice stepped in.

"BABY, PLEASE!!" I exclaimed.

I simply wanted to hear the truth from him, although I already knew the answer. I felt like how God must feel with us, He simply want for us to confess our sins, even though He knows them. Yet, my love stuck to his story and asked me where this was coming from. He accused a good friend of mine who had some concerns about why he was taking so long marrying me and making an excuse about a ring. She expressed her concerns to him, yet still he stuck to his guns. At this point, I was so glad this was over the phone not in person.

"Janetta Sutler, WHO IS SHE?" he was quiet.

"She is NOT your ex, she is your DAUGHTER, RIGHT!?"

He was still quiet.

I said, "I know someone who knows your daughter. Her name is not Jonaco, is it? The name that is on your arm?"

He softly said "No"

"You have told me for 10 years that your daughter is Jonaco even showing me the tatt on your arm the other night, when Jonaco is indeed your ex, RIGHT?"

I asked, "WHY have you lied to me all these years? I let you in, into my home, my heart, my family, why me?"

Before he could answer, I firmly said, "And you're still married?!"

He was caught. And because he didn't know the source or what I knew, he answered, "Unhuh!"

I screamed, "WHYYYYYYYYYYY???? HOWWWWWW could you do this to me, to us? I asked you OVER AND OVER, you made me think I was crazy! You have been lying to me for YEARS!! WHO ARE YOU?!"

He stated, "Baby, let me explain!"

"EXPLAIN!?!?!? I have been BEGGING you to EXPLAIN for YEARS, now that you are caught, you want to EXPLAIN? You know what I have been through, you PROMISED to protect me, you said God sent you! YOU ARE EVIL!! May God have mercy on you!"

Then, I hung up the phone.

It was bittersweet because I had confirmed he was a calculated LIAR, that he would do and say ANYTHING to protect his story, even if it meant hurting me, his LIE was protected!

I called my mom, "Mom, he is married. I knew something was not right."

"What are you going to do?" she asked.

I told her, "It's nothing I can do. I'm DONE. He has been deceiving me since we met over 10 years ago. I can't even be his friend now!"

The next day, I woke up with joy because again I was not crazy at all. I finally was obedient to God and not this LIAR. Again, he simply wanted to explain how a small lie became a greater one and he should have been honest. I told him that he doesn't have an honest bone in his body and that he will suffer because he lost a GOOD thing.

He begged for forgiveness; that is what he deserves, and it is the only way I will receive forgiveness, but that does not mean he has to be part of my life.

I cried all day; I was in disbelief. We were planning to marry the next year. We were planning to move to Orlando, Florida. Now everything had changed because he LIED, constantly.

I will heal, quickly, but the hardest part of it all is my son. He already lost his deceitful father (to death) while in my womb. This man knew this and helped me sort through it only to do the same thing.

Now, my son has lost not just one dad, but two. This could have all been avoided, had my *angel* had not been a devil in disguise. I know now to always trust my gut.

I pray to eventually get back up on that bike but will be more selective of the path I take to get to it. I will also be more mindful of the *meat* I consume as again, the bones that should have been spit out, may pass as meat, and just might choke the life out of you, if not careful.

"A toxic lover is someone damaged beyond repair."

Journey 11

Boy, You've Got Some Nerve

I met my person, or so I thought. When I met him, I was newly single with a baby. I was not looking to be in a relationship; I was just enjoying meeting people. He was handsome, and charismatic. We exchanged numbers that evening and said our good-byes. I enjoyed our meeting that evening and looked forward to speaking with him again.

See occasionally, I braided hair, and he was soon to be a client. It was around March and after a couple of appointments, I found myself really feeling this man. And it was obvious the feelings were mutual. We talked often and seemed to have a lot in common. He was refreshing after a difficult break up, and the more he came over for those hair appointments, the more I found myself liking where this was headed.

By May, we had gone on our first date. I was enjoying the phone calls before work, the late-night conversations about all the things we seemed to have in common. There was a connection, and it was truly electric. We dated for almost two years before he moved in with me. In that time, we had gone through all the steps in the aspect of getting to know each other so living with one another was the next obvious step...for us anyway.

He moved in with me about a year after I moved into my place. By this time, love had grown naturally. I loved him, I was in love with him, and I felt as though he loved me. We lived together for about eight years, and it was beautiful. We lived as a happy blended family. He has three daughters and I have four and they are all in the same peer group, so it worked out beautifully. We lived as adults going on about our everyday lives, raising daughters and laying out goals to crush the way couples do. I had fallen in love with someone who was my friend, my protector, my safe space, and my lover. I was looking forward to building our future together. Little did I know my whole entire world would come crashing down on me.

You see, somewhere in that eight-year time span, his feelings had changed. I discovered that he had been cheating. I do not know how long he had been cheating, but it was obvious that he had feelings for her because he had given her a nickname in his phone. At this point, I did not care how long it had been going on; I was devastated.

"When and where did we fall off the path?" was all I could think of as I cried for days. After those days of crying, I began to wonder *"What could we do to fix our relationship?"* The trust was broken but I was willing to do something I had never done and that was work to rebuild the trust. I loved this man, and I was willing to step outside of anything I had done before to work on this love we had built naturally.

I was under the impression he wanted this same thing. I had no clue I was about to be pushed to the pits of hell. My soul was about to be completely shattered. See, this man that I loved with all my heart and soul had not only cheated on me, but that infidelity brought about a tiny human. Yes, that's right, this man had a child with the other woman.

I was on a downward spiral, not only had this man cheated on me but he was out here having unprotected sex with another woman. This was simply beyond me because I thought he held our relationship to a higher standard. I assumed he held himself to a higher standard, but that simply was not the case. The love I thought we were both committed to was now a struggle for me to even see. I could not see past the disrespect that was being shown to the union by the one who told me *"Love grew and was not forced"* between us.

As all of this was happening, I had dealt with some personal struggles, but I was able to overcome those struggles. I had found out about this other child just after I had moved into my new apartment, so I tried to make a clean break. I was done, I had held my word and started to work on my healing. During this time, my brother from another mother was having some serious health issues. Unfortunately, he succumbed to his illness and my natural reaction was to call the one who was once my everything, everywhere, all at once.

Well, that threw me back into doing what I knew best, trying to find reason in the madness. So once again, after the apologies and the make-up sex and all the *"I'm committed to this..."* conversations, I was back in. I was trying to repair a situation I did not break. Things had not changed; in the way I felt, yet I was still in love. I could still see us salvaging this relationship and moving forward with our shared goals.

I honestly felt like he was sincere in his apologies, but I knew something was still off. He had not moved in with me, he barely spent the night, he would come by after work for a couple of hours, sometimes before work, we would still go out occasionally, I had even given him the key to the back door so he could come whenever he wanted but something still was not right. I did this dance with this man for another six years, until one day, it just clicked.

Thinking that you have found the love of your life, then finding out it was nothing more than narcissistic manipulation is a devastating blow. But there is beauty on the other side of healing. After six years, one day I just realized that this man used to go hard in the paint for me and now he was barely available to me. And from there it just went downhill, I have always known that love is something for everyone to experience and it should be healthy. This was no longer healthy. It was as though I was being demoted in my position as the "girlfriend" and I was not willing to participate in such foolery.

When I finally decided to walk away, I knew that challenging times were ahead. The shorter the text messages and phone calls got, the more tears I cried. I would randomly cry throughout the day. I could not control my emotions; I still loved this man so much. I had once told him that I would make myself unhappy before I allowed him to, and I meant that. And now I was here, in loneliness.

I had no clue how my heart would get over this, but I knew I was in this fight for my soul. As I said earlier, this time for me was different, I was older and just a tad bit wiser. My old methods of healing were to find myself in the arms of other men, normally someone I had no mental, physical, or emotional attachment to. This time my heart felt different, like it had been weakened in some aspect. Honestly speaking the only thing to do was find a way to heal.

The first couple of weeks were hard, I wanted to call, I wanted to text, and I wanted to ask him to come over so we could talk. But all those things had not worked previously. I had even drafted an email, said my goodbyes, and sent it before; but I went back after that, so it made no sense to do that again either. This time I had to go cold turkey, no contact, no matter how much I wanted to. When I tell you I cried for days on end, I cried every night. I had lost my mother a couple of years prior, but I longed for her energy and wisdom every minute of every day. One thing she had left me with was the knowledge that, no matter what, I was going to be okay.

So daily I got up and made every attempt to move forward and heal my own heart because no one had more to lose than me. See, at no time did this man give me an explanation for why he cheated on me, and looking back, his apologies were not genuine. Whatever had gone wrong in our situation was just left in the air, so I never knew what it was that I may have needed to improve upon.

I began to analyze myself; I know I am in no way perfect but where could I improve for me? I looked at all the positive things I bring to the table: I am a team player, I am an affectionate being, I love hugging and holding hands and spending quality time together. I have no problem cooking, cleaning, and taking on the role as the woman of the home. Then, I had to look at the issues that are not so healthy that I have. First, I spend money like I am a rich stay-at-home spouse, my consistency is not so consistent, I struggle with keeping my motivation going, but nevertheless, I still move forward. It was now time for me to move forward on my own and heal in a new way.

Honestly speaking, I am not all the way healed but I am better than I was when I walked away. Even though I still love this man, reality is that his love or lack thereof was no way real, not for me anyway. I wake up knowing that I am enough for me, and my constant evolution is what makes me better every day. My heart is meant to love, and it will again one day, but for now healing comes by learning to love all the parts of me that are great and not so great.

Loving the journey itself has become important, I appreciate the woman I am. The mother in me is phenomenal and that shows in the four amazing daughters that I have raised. I had to walk away from everything that I knew to find my path again. The truth is that my methods of healing before were in no way forms of healing, but this go round, it has been different because I put myself first.

I love the space I currently reside in; I have been with myself for a while now and I am simply fine with that. It works for me, as I work on my dreams. I have accomplished a couple of the things on my bucket list, and I am going for the rest of them. One of them is to do just what I am doing now, letting people know that there is life on the other side of a healed heart. The love and the light that comes with living in your own truth is so extremely powerful. Every day we have the opportunity for a blessing or a lesson, it is on us to determine which is which.

I know the best is yet to come because I do the work to heal, beautiful self- talk, positive affirmations, self- care rituals all are important when it comes to healing. All are good for the mind, body, and soul. Every step on this side of heartbreak has been worth it because this journey has shown me things about me that I had forgotten. These days the first thing I do is forgive myself, take accountability, and check my emotions. The focus is on healing my way, every way possible. Changing one's perspective is a fantastic way to switch energy in any situation and that's what I did.

"If a person disregards your feelings, ignores your needs, and treats you in a damaging way, distance yourself."

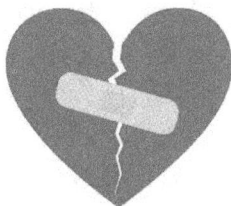

Journey 12

Not Gon Cry

Years later, I can see why God allowed all this to happen. I will be forever grateful for my daughter. I do not regret having her, I just wish it wasn't with this man-child. He's in his 50's now and this fool is still ran by his mother.

Our relationship lasted over a period of five years. I didn't get pregnant until we had already broken up. His mother told me to stop calling, and that I was lying about the pregnancy. I regret that I was moving backwards in life not knowing that I would be connected to this fool and his mother forever.

I came across this talent show event being held at a nearby club and thought it would be a great opportunity for me to show off my singing and stage performance skills, so I signed up. There I was, on stage performing Mary J. Blige's song, "Not Gon Cry." Little did I know, I would later be singing this same song but with a whole lot of heart behind it.

He was so handsome standing near the bar holding

his drink with his pinky finger out looking all fly. He was 6'3" medium built and definitely worked out. He had what we called "good hair," smooth dark skin, and I remember noticing his lips. Those lips had me fantasizing about what he could do with them.

Getting off the stage, there he was to congratulate me on my performance. His mother walks over and she was actually one of the DJ's who was a part of the radio station that put the show together. He introduced us and I thought to myself, "*Wow - a man that loves his mother!*" They appeared to be so close with each other. Little did I know, she ran the show of his life.

The talent show ended early, but I didn't want the night to end. We had a few drinks, or maybe more than a few. To be honest, alcohol was a major problem in both our lives at that time.

As the night continued, we laughed and slow danced. He made me feel special that night. He could have chosen anyone, but he chose me. That Hennessey had me in LaLa Land.

I don't really know when the cheating started. I think he was a player from the start. His mother knew before me, but of course she never told me anything. Their relationship was kind of strange. She bottled fed that nigga and still does until today. Still, knowing how much she interfered in our relationship, I still agreed to move in with him, and his mother of course. We lived upstairs and shared the common areas.

Everything was fine.... until he wasn't coming home at night, sometimes not until the next morning. I knew it had to be another woman. We all know what happens in the streets during those hours of the night.

I would drive myself crazy, losing sleep and calling

his phone over and over again, text after text and no answer. Now here I go barely and by the grace of God , missed a life sentence in one of Louisiana's finest women's prison. I recall the rage and anger I felt because his punk ass wasn't answering my calls or text. This was happening way too much, and I decided to do something about it.

I got in my car, leaving quietly and calmly so I wouldn't wake his nosey mama. I went out looking for his ass and if I saw this bitch it was over for the both of them. This town wasn't very big; one way in, one way out kind of city. The FBI had nothing on me finding him, and I did just that.

How lucky I was to see his black Cadillac drive right in front of me. I saw the chick riding on the passenger side. At this point, I checked out and was ready for whatever. I decided to run them off the road. I proceeded and pointed my pistol at him. By the grace of God, he got away and I escaped the plans of the enemy. The reason I say that is because I would have been under the prison, and at this time my daughter wasn't born yet.

Fast forward to a few years later, I thought just maybe we could be friends with benefits. I ended up getting pregnant. He didn't believe me, of course. I called him and told him that I had the ultrasound. His mother got on the phone and told me to stop lying and harassing him. There I went again, trying to love a man who never had love for me.

My water broke and I was on the phone with my homegirl who was miles away but so supportive, telling me to get my butt in the car and get to the hospital. I had no family nearby, no one.

I thought I had time to do my hair and makeup she

said, "Girl, stop! You're a natural and you about to have that baby at home if you don't leave now!"

I got in my car, my friend stayed on the phone with me all the way to the hospital. I drove myself to Oshner Medical Center. I parked and started walking towards the emergency room where the security officer spotted me right away.

He said, "Ma'am, wait right there. Let me get you a wheelchair."

I was in labor, ready to deliver. The doctor was there and two female nurses.

The doctor asked, "Where's everybody?"

I replied, "It's just us Doc," as I swallowed hard to keep my tears from choking me.

One of the nurses came to my side, grabbed my hand, and said, "Baby, you are not alone. God is with you and will always be every step of the way."

That nurse stood by me the whole time. Minutes later, my beautiful baby girl arrived.

It took me some time to mentally heal but I did, and I became stronger. After this point, nothing mattered to me most but getting myself together and leaving this man behind. If he had ever decided to come around, that's fine. If he decided to never speak to me or be here for our daughter, that would be fine also. I knew in my spirit it was time to say Boy BYE!. I had enough and I went through labor without him, so I knew I was strong enough for whatever was next.

"A healthy relationship will never require you to sacrifice your friends, your dream, or your dignity."

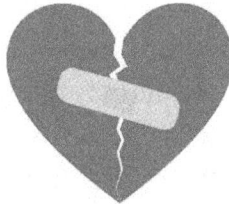

Journey 13

How Many Times

It was August of 2005. I was in the process of moving into a new apartment. This was a welcomed change for me and my two children, ages nine and three. I was a single mother looking for a break because financially I needed something more affordable and needed much more space for my children to grow. This move seemed like the perfect opportunity to get what we needed, and I was happy to be able to provide for our little family.

Being a single mother is not an easy task, but I did the best that I could with whatever I had. The new apartment needed a new refrigerator, and the apartment manager quickly made it happen. She asked another tenant to help bring in the refrigerator and this is when he and I had our first encounter.

Love at first sight is not actually the best way to describe it. There was definitely a connection between the two of us. I did not know that eventually there would be more to this story, but when do we ever know what the future holds?

A few days went by and I was at a local store shopping when I ran into my next door neighbor. She informed me that the guy that had helped move my new refrigerator was inquiring about my number, but she was hesitant to give out the information. She took his number instead to give to me and I contemplated whether I should call him or not.

Eventually, I did call, and we had a good conversation, but I was not sold on the idea of having someone new in my life and around my children. I found out a day later that my oldest brother knew of this guy and my brother spoke very highly of him. They had played arena football together, so I trusted my big brother and let my guard down. I became more open to dating him.

Everything started off very nice and I was happy to have someone I could talk to and see every single day. We grew closer and closer. I really trusted him to the point I would let him drive my red 1997 (5-speed) Mitsubishi Mirage Coupe. This was a big deal because this was my first car and I never let anyone drive my car other than my little brother and my dad. I am not a materialistic person, but I was protective of what I had because my car was my livelihood to and from work or wherever I needed to take my children. To trust him with my prized possession (Redbug) meant I had really fallen for him and from here there was no turning back.

In September of 2005, we were officially a couple and my children seemed to like him as well. He had three girls of his own that lived in different cities and states. We talked about him spending more time with them in the near future. As I think back, there may have been a red flag or two or maybe even 3. But I was giving him the benefit of the doubt, which I no longer do when I see people for who they truly are. Nothing seemed out of the ordinary and I did not have any concerns because he seemed to be what I needed at that time. He did all the right things in the beginning and everything else I felt would get better as time progressed.

In February of 2006, I found out that I was pregnant. This news caught me by surprise. I know I was not protecting myself responsibly at the time, so I was okay and accepted the consequences of my actions. Fast forward to June 2006, we decided to get married, and I was happy because I really did not want to bring another child into the world without doing it traditionally. My first two children were born out of wedlock and to be married this time would be better than to not be married at all.

After getting married, things started going downhill. I did not realize that I would be in for the ride of my life. One day, while I was sitting on my porch, I was approached by my husband's aunt, and I knew something was wrong. She wanted to let me know that my husband was not being faithful. For some reason, I did not get upset or angry. I was four or five months pregnant at this time and I cannot say that this news did not hurt, but something in me did not react as I thought I would have.

My phone rang. It was my husband's grandmother who was upset that the aunt had come to my home with what she called "mess." Yes, it was a mess that your grandson created, and this was the bed he would soon have to lie in.

In October of 2006, on Friday the 13th, our beautiful daughter was born. I was very happy because I was able to experience what I did not have when I gave birth to my first and second child. Things did not get better after our daughter was born, but I still tried to stick to my marriage vows.

There were things that I could not unsee and the fact that he possessed two cell phones added to the other red flags I had collected and stashed away. This was not a big deal since he had been running his own car wash business and from there he began painting buildings and whatever else people needed. There were so many things that I overlooked because he was my husband, but I just knew that it would get better with time.

As time went on, he acquired multiple cars and even had a motorcycle that I did not approve of. But later I would realize how all this came about and how naïve I was when it came to this whole situation. I did find proof of his infidelity and the way that I found out was devastating. I will only say that it could have affected me in a physical way but thank God it did not, and it was resolved on his behalf. Whoever is reading this may think that I am foolish at this point because this latest episode should have been the last. But there I was choosing to forgive my husband, once again, and trying to hold on to what I promised God I would do.

After I found out about my husband's infidelity, it seemed that he wanted to work on our marriage and do what was right by our family. We did have our new baby and two other children in the house, so we were trying to be a better example for them. One thing I have learned is that you cannot make someone do right because that person has to want to do right on their own.

In July of 2008, my husband lost his oldest brother in a tragic car accident, which affected him a great deal in so many ways. We even started going to church and I thought we were going on the right path, but I was so wrong and misled. Anyone would have thought that this tragic situation would have changed my husband for the better, but things only got worse.

The next episode is like a lifetime movie that I cannot believe I went through and came out sane. I cannot believe I had not walked away a lot sooner, but I just wanted my marriage to work and live up to the promises that we had made. I now know that marriage cannot be a one-way street because you have to have two people willing to work towards the same goals. No matter how bad I wanted my marriage to work and prayed for my husband to do right, it had to be a mutual commitment.

January of 2009 is a year I will never forget because I was headed for a detour that I did not see coming. There were a lot of things that I was blind to that hit me in the face with a force I could not understand. My husband was leaving the house to go hang out with some friends, which was normal and nothing out of the ordinary. As usual, our daughter wanted to tag along with her dad, but he reassured her that he would be back. She got the idea of her going with him out of her mind and her attention turned towards playing with her older sister and brother. He left the house, and I went about my normal routine of taking care of my children and preparing things for the next day.

Nighttime came and I had put my children to bed. I decided to get on the computer (MySpace) until my husband came home. The phone rang a little after nine and it was my husband saying that he had been arrested and was in the city jail. I thought that he was joking, so I kept asking when he was coming home but he insisted that he was telling me the truth. I still thought that he was joking with me until he asked me to call his mom. Right then and there I knew that this was real and not a joke like I had thought.

My world was being turned upside down in a matter of minutes and I was at the point of not knowing what to do. I called his mom but there was nothing we could do besides wait until the morning to see exactly what had happened. My nightmare had begun, and I wish I could've awakened from this dream. It would only worsen as the events of the whole truth began to unfold.

What I had not explained earlier in this story is that my husband was a convicted felon who had been convicted of dealing drugs years before I had met him. Everyone deserves a second chance, but he still had not learned his lesson because he was still doing the same thing. I found out that during our whole marriage he was involved in illegal activities that also included income tax fraud. I could not believe all of this was happening right under my nose and I absolutely had no clue. God has a way of revealing things even when you do not want to see them.

The night he got arrested he was in his mistress's car which had a gun in it and was against his probation as a felon. To find this out after everything else I had been through just broke me down to my knees. Yet again I tried to stand by him, but I was becoming very worn down because this was my husband that I loved him, but he was not loving me like he was supposed to be. I began to question God about why this was happening to me because I was doing my best to be the wife I thought I should be. Sometimes we as women have to understand that it has absolutely nothing to do with us but everything to do with the other person and their inability to love us correctly.

Eventually, I could not take it anymore because it was affecting me as a woman and as a mother. The last straw that brought me to reality was when I was checking out at the local Walmart and a man asked me if my daughter was mine. I told him yes and he proceeded to tell me that he knew her dad and one day followed him to our home. There was a look of shock upon my face because I could not believe what I was hearing, and I knew then that God had protected me and my children the whole time. The man continues to tell me how my husband had owed him money and that he followed him that day to "get" him for stealing from him. The only thing that saved my husband was the fact that our daughter was with him, and I knew then that it was God who had intervened. All I could do was stand there and listen because I could not believe what was coming out of his mouth.

I paid for my groceries and quickly left because how could someone be so comfortable with telling me this. I never really understood how much danger my kids and I were in from the drugs he was dealing, his car being stolen and shot into, FBI agents, DEA agents, and unknown people that were after my husband. All I know is that I had to get out of this situation because it was too dangerous for me and my children to continue living in.

I filed for a divorce and never looked back because I knew it was the best thing for me and my children. I moved in with my mother and tried to make things as normal as possible, but it was hard after all of the chaos and stress. Today, we co-parent our 17-year-old daughter and I have forgiven my ex-husband for putting me and my children through pure hell and all of the drama. There is a domino effect that I did not think of as a mother or he as a dad when it came to the children in the situation as a whole. I am thankful to God that the situation had no lasting effects on my children mentally and emotionally.

I do not regret anything that I went through because God covered me and my three through it all. To end the marriage was bittersweet but the best decision I ever made. The only regret I have is allowing my young children to experience the pain and confusion of everything that they had no control over. What I have also learned from this is to stop collecting red flags because one red flag is ONE too many. When a person shows you who they truly are, "BELIEVE" them and not what you perceive or want them to be. I would not be who I am or where I am today without God and his covering over our lives. I am thankful after all that we have been through to truly understand the gift in saying Boy BYE!

"If you walked away from a toxic, negative, abusive, one-sided, dead-end, low vibrational, relationship or friendship – you won."

Journey 14

El Lesbiana

It felt like I watched my heart slowly break as the events unfolded. I watched the rage ignite like that of a lit cigarette, then when not careful I watched the flame grow stronger and hotter before my eyes could blink. Obviously I could see that all I had to do was blow out the small flame before it spread to a full-blown fire, but what if I told you I was addicted to the sting of the fire? Would you think I was crazy?

Have you ever been in love with someone you are affectionately attracted to? The flutter of butterflies in the pit of your stomach, when they're close to you, when they say your name, or when you share the same space as them, creates special memories you both can bring back to life at any second just to relive the sweet moment. This is the motivation I commonly used to love my lover, my sweet El Lesbiana, a little bit more as I loved myself a little less.

After what I had experienced before meeting my

love, I had little trust in people. If a person showed me who they truly were, I would forgive, but I wouldn't allow people to burn me twice. I had compassion and patience yet had a backbone. I searched my soul daily to find the missing woman whose cut-off game was sharper than a two-edged sword, but the woman I used to be was now the invisible lady.

What in the ham & cheese is going on?! Who am I? As I looked back at myself in my bathroom mirror, I didn't even recognize who was looking back at me. My eyes had aged, and the wrinkles had begun to show under my eyes due to years of non-stop crying from a broken heart. I was in a state of emotional distress during this relationship. It began as a slow brewing rollercoaster ride that had sent chills through my body, butterflies in the pit of my stomach and my heart accelerated due to the thrill of this new romantic connection. I was on top of the world. I can't explain how good it feels to establish a connection with someone; it's like a long-anticipated wait from someone you'd least expect but expected.

I don't want to be brash over specific events, but I want to share the very important ones so that you follow along with ease and understanding. I fell in love with El Lesbiana at the tender age of 16. We met at the age of 15. In case it hasn't clicked, El Lesbiana is a woman. The purpose of any lesbian relationship is not only being physically and sexually attracted to a woman but it's also being attracted emotionally to a woman. The soft edge of a woman, the emotional intelligence of a woman that no man can execute. This was my whole purpose of being involved with a woman. However, I eventually discovered, that it was like being in a relationship with a man. Not to say all men are like what I am about to describe, but the emotional intelligence that I craved appeared to be found in the initial getting-to-know-you phase but was later abandoned.

The soft, gentle El Lesbiana who carried on conversations, and romanticized being together at a moment's notice slowly faded into a self-absorbed abusive woman. Her lovely features that beheld her beauty scared me like that of a phantom hiding in the dark. What's considered more alarming? Slowly breaking someone's heart in a thousand pieces over and over with each time being more insidious than the last one? Or perhaps being led into a false sense of security to exploit your vulnerabilities to use them as ammunition to later betray your sense of emotional well-being and self-trust?

We spent every day together like a Bonnie & Clyde dynamic, getting in trouble, drinking, partying under the sun. The two of us together were a force, but an explosive force mixed with intense passion and a firepower of consequences that still haunt me until this day. We were young lovers, but both of us had to grow up into adults before our time which is why teenage love interested us very much. We had a chance to be young and not adults, to laugh, to cry, to have fun, and to not think or be concerned with mere consequences. But everything you do in this life has a consequence, good, bad, or indifferent and consequences do not always follow right after an action, sometimes consequences of our actions show up later in our lives.

The consequence of ignoring red flags in a relationship sometimes has irreversible consequences and sometimes deadly ones. There is no such thing as overacting in a toxic relationship. Your bones confirm you're in a toxic relationship, your gut confirms you're in a toxic relationship, your mind confirms you're in a toxic relationship, but your heart is holding onto hope of repairing the relationship. Being led into a false sense of security is an insidious process. For example, think of it as being led into a beautiful house, there are beautiful decorations on the inside, nice décor, the ease of being welcomed home safely, and unbeknownst to you, a wolf is waiting to devour you in this beautiful nightmare. The disheartening part is, you're in love with the wolf and you are hoping if you love the wolf enough, it may turn into a sheep; soft, authentic, compassionate, and vulnerable. Imagine going through this cycle over and over again as you're being emotionally manipulated to believe that you are the one who holds the burden of restoring the relationship to what it once was. This is a lie. It's a lie because it takes two to tango and not just one person. In any relationship worth saving, both parties bear the burden of repairing it.

As I was slowly, emotionally, and mentally manipulated, the physical abuse came right after. As I reached my twenties, the intensity of our sour relationship took flight in the worst way. One night spent with her and some of her associated friends, she had been drinking and drinking beyond legal. Her attitude was that of a drunken rage that made me tread lightly on what I said or did. As I watched the inflections in her voice, I wanted to comfort her. Some of us have had moments where we are drunk, and we reflect on some things in our lives that bring us to tears. This is what was happening with El Lesbiana.

As I attempted to console her as she sat next to me on the bed with a reassuring voice of validation, this tone I used angered her.

"Don't talk to me like that. Don't talk to me like I am a baby. I'm not a bitch, I'm strong," El Lesbiana said.

"I am not talking to you like a baby. I just want to reassure you that I am here for you," I replied.

In a quick second, she pushed me onto the bed. My body was laid flat on my back. She straddled herself on top of me as she sat her weight on my stomach and upper legs so that I could not move. I struggled to get free as I wailed my arms in the air, attempting to lift my body weight from off the bed to hopefully get her off of me. In this room that we were in was a guest room, and the door was closed. As I attempted to yell for her to get off of me, within a split second, she took the small pillow that lay idle next to me and placed it firmly onto my face. She pressed down slightly and for a moment or two, I couldn't breathe. I don't know where this voice came from, but I heard a still small voice say, *'Don't wail your arms. Don't panic. If you do, she will press down harder. Be calm and she will lift the pillow.'* I did as the voice said. I calmed my body and didn't wail my arms any longer. I was petrified that she would continue to smother me, but I was relieved when she lifted the pillow off of my face.

I was scared of what she had just done. I was confused about what made her do this to me, and I was afraid of what might happen next if I overreacted. I decided to remain calm because it was important to keep her calm so that nothing else would happen. Once the shock had worn off between the both of us, she eventually told me she did not mean it. She told me it was a joke and not to be melodramatic about it. She looked at it as a joke, but I didn't. If she had continued to press down any longer, I could have lost consciousness. My gut was telling me I was in danger, but my heart screamed

"Your love can change her." Looking back at things now, my love couldn't change her at all. You can love a person so much, but the only two people who can change a grown person are God and the person who wants to change. If I had conceived this truth, the other events wouldn't have unfolded.

Throughout the years, after the pillow incident, things gradually became worse. Physical violence not only took place in private but had taken place in public quite a few times. It is embarrassing to be hurt and attacked by the one you love in private, but even more embarrassing in public. To see onlookers watching you be hurt by someone who says they love you is jaw-dropping. You feel this intense fear of not only being judged by onlookers but also extreme fear of the possibility of your life ending at the hands of someone who promised to cherish it. Being picked up by a woman and man-handled, being thrown across a parking lot, with multiple strikes to the head and my head being slammed into the pavement is horrendous. I had no control over that relationship. El Lesbiana had the power, I was just simply being driven into mental oblivion. An absolute mental state of despair, rot, sadness, and helplines.

The relationship went to a homerun when a love triangle ensued between El Lesbiana, a new woman, and me. This love triangle took place for twelve years of the eighteen years she and I were together. The love triangle had anything but love in it. Two souls competing for one's affection is an insidious process. A love triangle is a psychological threesome that you did not consent to. I did not consent to the love triangle; I wanted my dear El Lesbiana. I wanted her to trade in her wolf tendencies for sheepish ways. I waited so long to see my hope come to fruition. For my labored love, I dreamed of a harvest with her. But just like the thunder hitting the ground and my garden of love, it was destroyed. Never to be the same again. This is the coming-of-age realization one comprehends when God says it's time to wake up.

The moment I had finally been waiting for had arrived. The moment of clarity, strength, wittiness, and mental reform. It felt like wool had been lifted from my eyes. Suddenly, I could see me! I was no longer the invisible lady. My backbone started to grow like limbs on a tree, and oh boy did it grow back strong. I didn't crave any validation or acceptance from El Lesbiana, I checked myself for it. The validation, the care, the compassion, the love, the understanding I sought, I decided to give it to myself. Loving myself was just as important as loving others.

Over time, I am learning to be graceful towards myself, to exercise self-compassion for my not knowing things or not seeing things in a clearer view. I am still learning how to forgive myself for not knowing my worth and my value. Through this experience, I am more patient with myself in learning things as they come, accepting the things that I cannot change, the courage to change the things I can, and the wisdom to know the difference.

The consequences of staying in that relationship longer than I should have were emotional and mental. The anxiety caused me to be in a state of emotional and mental distress for long periods. I am hypervigilant of my surroundings, of people, and even some opportunities. My extrovert personality where I was social with people has simmered down to whereas I prefer my own company or at least safe company. I haven't given up on love, but I am careful of who I fall in love with. I also understand that the very things that I was criticized about, taunted about, accused of being overfriendly to others, too caring, too naïve, the very things that El Lesbiana did not like about me are the very things that someone else would gladly appreciate. The great qualities, the good parts of you that one doesn't like about you are answered prayers for someone else out there looking to meet you. This experience taught me really hard lessons but taught me precious things as well.

God has made me into His image. I do not apologize for how creatively, genuinely, and imperfect he has made me. I do not apologize for anything except for not knowing my self-worth. The purpose of sharing parts of my story is because I want to give those hope who find themselves stuck in abusive relationships. With no rhyme or reason, we all may not discover the real reason or a satisfying one as to why abusers abuse those whom they say they love. However, we have everything we need to treat others with love, respect, compassion, and understanding. Just because someone has had a hard day at work doesn't give them the right to abuse another person to let off steam, or just because someone has had a harsh upbringing doesn't give them the right to abuse others. Abuse is not love and love is not abuse. Sometimes abusers do not reveal their tactics until you're emotionally involved, and time has been invested, and on the other hand, some abusers show you initially. Either way, an abuser's goal is to obtain and maintain power and control.

Abusers do not look at people as people, but mere objects. I leave this with you, get to know people as much as you can at a comfortable pace. Actively listen, be prepared to ask questions, and observe how a person responds when life happens or when things do not work in their favor. Observe how they treat others. Pay close attention to red flags because your life may depend on it.

"A bad relationship is like standing on broken glass, if you stay you will keep hurting. If you walk away, you will hurt but eventually, you will heal."

Journey 15

The Gap Between Us

Pastor Grady cleared his throat. He seemed to act as if was busy or in a meeting. He quickly responded.

"I took your name off the paperwork to the church and the youth board."

I interrupted, "Wait, why?"

Squinting my eyes at the cell phone trying to put it on the speaker but couldn't. So, I continued to question what I called for.

"Why leave me working all these years? Me thinking I was a part of something that I'm not! I worked so hard for...," I inhaled.

He kept going on about his unprofessional sense of betrayal and how he let his pride get in the way of our endeavors.

My feelings started to take control. I said to myself, *"No! First Lady remain calm."*

Letting out an exhale as his voice irritated my soul over the phone. I thought about standing as a wife and First Lady submissively to Pastor Grady at one point in our marriage. I played a pivotal role, making the church and him look good in the community and public's eyes. But now I'm here just listening.

As he spoke with authority over every aspect of the church operations, I found myself in the crossfire of my hard work and dedication. I was overlooked once again because of his power play.

I put my ear to the phone, drained by his voice. He continued.

"I won't discredit you from being the visionary of the organization, and the First Lady of the congregation."

I was perplexed. I spoke over his words.

"First Lady? Are you kidding me? We are divorcing! I'm not going to keep pretending to the congregation Pastor Grady," I said sternly.

He cleared his voice to continue.

"Umm umm...However, your job as the COO to the church organization isn't on the paperwork as of 2018."

I sighed and replied, "But we started it together in 2017, it's MY vision!"

I paused. Then, I proceeded to ask the question I already knew the answer to.

"So, you stab me in the back a year later? Wow!"

I was in disbelief and disappointed. I raised my eyebrow at my cell phone, turning it towards me to put him on speaker, as I paced the room I was in.

A sista tried to keep calm, but my heart's blood started to rush with rage. I could feel the tears coming from the bottom of my belly because of the pain. I answered myself out loud.

"So, you let me build you up, and the organization, while you sat on your ass for almost eleven years? And waited six years later to do this?!"

He didn't answer. So, I continued without breaking. "It's 2023 now!" I announced.

His voice elevated, responding back to my own answered questions.

"I don't give a damn, my church, my operation, my rules!" he firmly stated and chuckled. "Now, go wear your pants somewhere else because I wear the pants here!"

He was talking like someone was in front of him, like he was trying to impress by throwing his authority to me over the phone.

I could imagine that gap in his mouth. And at that moment, our eight-year age gap was displayed in his immaturity of communicating, and not being honest.

My dad warned me about it before he handed me over to him on our wedding day. His words replayed quickly

"You sure you wanna do this?" My dad asked. "Yes!" I said happily, looking like the belle of the ball as he and I walked down the aisle. *"Why do you ask that Daddy?"* He held my hand close to his heart. *"He's a liar."* I heard my dad say it before, but I chose to ignore it. I saw the red flags.

As my dad and I swayed down the aisles, I shook my head with a smile. I reminded my dad about his own theory and asked. *"Why daddy because of the gap in his mouth?"* I was being sarcastic.

My dad chuckled. I laughed as we almost approached my groom at the time. I caught my dad by replying, *"Momma has a gap."* He stared at me with one stern eye. *"People who have gaps tell the most lies."* We both laughed.

As he gave me to Mr. Terance Grady, my dad whispered in my ear, *"Watch that bridge."*

He played it off with a kiss on my cheek. I giggled into my then husband's hand to say I do.

I reminisce about that day and what my dad said. It was clear. I became more annoyed. I jolted my head back and muted my phone quickly so that I could call Pastor Grady every name but a child of God!

I began a reassurance prayer for myself.

As I yelled, "Lord, I stayed a steadfast, devoted advocate of the community and congregation. I poured my heart into building and believing in his ministry for the youth. Please, Lord give me the right words to say to this negro at this point."

Pastor Grady wanted to go back and forth with the conversation and be argumentative over this mess he caused. So, I zoned out... thinking of everything that occurred in our relationship over the years. I felt so used up! I was battling with my left and right shoulder, the devil and angel. Trying not to lose my composure. But all I knew was the facts.

One big fact I remember was the years that we didn't have money coming in together with four kids, two adults, and just one household income. So, I found a second job at Los Angeles International Airport (LAX), cleaning toilets to make ends meet while Pastor Grady sat home until it was time to go to church. I worked my fingers to the bone, literally, even making sure the youth kept fundraisers every month. (The church was supposed to be run based on donations towards the youth music, and dance ministries.)

Once the church started running in with donations, his selfish habits of wanting to indulge himself in a lavish lifestyle kicked in while neglecting core values of prioritizing in household finances. On the other hand, I started looking busted, chipped nail polish, hair looking crazy, and toes were on hammer time, the household bills were behind with shut off notices. Hell, I would rather look crazy before my bills aren't paid, and we get put out of our place, instead of us waiting on the Pastors, waiting until the members' dues and donations were paid, so he would be able to pay a household bill. Not including the church bills. By that time most of the bills were shut off or they became delinquent, and he had to get caught up to pay them, then we were back broke. Well, at least I was. In the course of our marriage, his money was his money.

I unmuted the phone ready to retaliate. I utterly returned.

"Boy BYE!"

I broke down into tears and my emotions raged. I couldn't listen to him say another word, so I hung up the phone. I couldn't take it anymore. The rooted pride between us both conflicted with the mission and the vision for the youth in the community. He became complacent and allowed me to wear the pants in the marriage, and the organization. Things that I prioritized in place, he sat and snagged it up underneath my feet.

Before I found out about Pastor taking my name off the church deed, and the organization, I had become depressed and still tried to get back into my routine of being productive and happy. Still maintaining the youth program and concerts. Our marriage was already in shambles; we stayed together but separately. East and West wing of the house.

I began to regain my focus back into myself as Golden and not the First Lady that was standing on the Pastor's arm as a trophy. Now, the hustling me was back. I went back into health & beauty making and selling soap like it was crack! Me and my girl Logic who was at the time a member of our congregation and organization as the CFO. We made good online money and connections around the world! We had people who brought our products from overseas. Facebook became our platform. *"Relax, Relate, and Release"* was our slogan and the social media fans couldn't wait until we were back on live doing something amusing.

Our youth modeled our apparel helping to sell our products. They even performed online to keep our audience engaged. The kids are so talented that people would give to them from their bosom without us being in a church. And that's how they made their own money.

We had it all together. At least I thought. Until Covid hit our church home taking out nearly half the members of the congregation. Even our beloved Bishop and Youth Minister went home to glory, leaving Grady and I to pick up the rest of the pieces, which were big shoes to fill at the time. No one knew that Grady and I were separated.

Years of us pretending for the members and the community started to play out. Pastor started to get desperate, getting PPP loans on the organization, without Logic (CFO) or my consent (COO). When he did mention it to us, we both disagreed because we both knew the consequences of it. However, it was too late, and Pastor Grady had proceeded with the transaction.

He received a hundred thousand dollars from the loan and was barely paying the staff and me. Ok, wait, he paid me rent – for what it's worth. Well, eventually the government wanted the money back from the loan.

The pandemic was taking family members left and right! If you had a cold or sniffles you were subjected to the deadly virus. Unfortunately, it hit home for me. My mom passed away due to kidney failure. I had to run to the state of Texas and get my mom together. At the time, the Pastor and I were on the rim of divorce.

I took off a year from the organization and Logic had to as well with the passing of her beloved dad. I stayed in Texas getting the farm together that my mom left behind for us. My heart was heavy, and my mind couldn't focus clearly enough to get back to normal. Even with the church, Pastor knew I was coming back to build my part of the organization. I just needed a little more time. My mom was gone for Christ's sake. He didn't even waste time on moving forward while I was gone. The organization and church belonged to both of us I thought. But before I knew it, he had already taken me off the paperwork a year after we coordinated the program with my vision. And now we're here in this predicament.

Pastor Grady didn't have any empathy; he felt the show must go on at that moment; the organization was his only source of income. So, life went on he felt in his world. But my world stopped for me. Losing a parent is hard, not easy to bounce back from. I told him that I needed time, and it would help if he could look over the youth events and affairs while I was away. All the time he wanted me out of the way.

Before Covid-19 ended, I had the brutal courage to start my own alliance against Pastor Grady. I'm proceeding to continue my vision for the youth program beyond the church walls, aiming still to secure scholarships for underprivileged and at promised youth needs in the community. I was faced with unexpected obstacles because of the male ego of Pastor Grady; he thought I was going to fall by making the gap between us.

Boy BYE! You're right, I wear the pants you gave me to wear...

"At some point you have to realize that some people can stay in your heart but not in your life."

Journey 16

Untitled

You think you can talk to me any kind of way - Boy BYE! You think you can disrespect me in front of others - Boy BYE! You think that you can disrespect me behind closed doors - Boy BYE! You yell at me in front of your family and friends and they act like it doesn't happen - Boy BYE!

Your bro said, "Well she won't leave him-she still with him." Really? - Boy BYE! You think I'm weak when I know that I'm strong - Boy BYE! You travel, I'm good with it. I travel, you upset - Boy BYE! You drive my cars like you runnin in a rat race but want someone to drive yours like Barack Obama is sitting in the back. - Boy BYE!

You tell lies and expect everyone to believe them - Boy BYE! You think you know what is best for me, and you thought wrong - Boy BYE! You think we are *friends*? You really thought so? - Boy BYE! You talk about my friends because they see the truth, when your friends still see the lies - Boy BYE!

Your actions in the world made you look like you provided for your family - Boy BYE! You act like you were taught well to be a man - Boy BYE! You think you are the best partner in the world - Boy BYE! You think that you are the best thing that ever happened to me - Boy BYE!

You think you know what love is - Boy BYE! You think you can judge me and compare me to others - Boy BYE! You said, "You don't make a $100,000," and I said, "You don't either!" - Boy BYE! You think you are in your winning season because you look like you have it together for once with your knock offs! Who you foolin? - Boy BYE!

You think that you can use my past against my present and future - Boy BYE! You think that you can disrespect me by my family actions - Boy BYE! You say you believe in God, but your actions show that you believe in a god - Boy BYE!

Farewell because I found someone who loves me for me, who cares for me, who has always been waiting for me to return. Someone who is such a gentleman and who has promised me that HE will never leave me nor forsake me.

HE has been there through it all - all that I've been through with you. HE continues to wait on the sidelines until I return to HIM. HE is first now.

HE was there when you had me in tears and quickly wanted to rush in but since HE is such a gentleman HE waited until I was ready to return to HIM. I'm so grateful that HE is there for me. HE tucks me in at night and wakes me up just in time for work. HE provides for me on a daily basis. So, Boy BYE! God is and was always the best thing that has ever happen to me.

"The moment that you start to wonder if you deserve better, you do."

ABOUT THE ANTHOLOGIST

Tanya Denise is the Founder & Executive Director of the International Association of Women Authors (IAWA), the world's leading global network for women who write. She is a self-published, international, best-selling author, anthologist, publisher, and writing coach. Born Latanya Hampton, in Pasadena, California, Tanya has been writing since she was a young girl, beginning her journey with poetry and short stories, then gradually growing into award winning essays, newsletters, newspapers, independent magazines, journals, then books.

Tanya is a serial entrepreneur, and she is a certified Domestic Violence Specialist. Her first anthology series titled, *Pretty Sad* includes five volumes of stories about the extraordinary strength of women who have overcome trauma, including abuse, addiction, depression, prostitution, and more. *Pretty Sad* is the first book series under the #timetotell movement. The movement was created by Tanya to create a space for women to tell their stories of going from tragedy to triumph! *Pretty Sad* was the #1 new release on Amazon in December 2019 and became a best seller!

In 2018, Tanya founded Love Wins Publishing (www.lovewinspub.com), to assist new and aspiring female writers in becoming published authors. She has published more than 55 of her own books, including journals, anthologies, workbooks, self-help books, devotionals, and her memoir. In addition, Tanya has helped more than 400 writers become first-time published authors.

In 2023, Tanya founded Writer's Block Press (WBP), (www.writersblockpress.com) and now oversees multiple publishing companies. WPB is an emerging publishing house that aims to revolutionize the world of literature and bring forth a new era of literary excellence. The company serves writers of all ages and demographics.

Tanya has a heart for helping others. Her passion has led to the receipt of several community awards, including Woman of the Year by the Antelope Valley Ad Hoc Committee on Education. Tanya's purpose is to utilize her proven faith in God to serve as a catalyst to help others heal and operate in their gift(s). Her mission is to use her gift of writing to help and empower individuals to walk in their purpose.

With a passion for finance, Tanya is a licensed insurance agent, and she enjoys traveling, spending time with her loved ones, and trying new restaurants. Tanya is an enthusiastic writer, speaker, and book coach. She is a mother of two and currently resides in Southern California.

For speaking engagements, bulk book orders, publishing services, and or more information, please visit:

www.authortanyadenise.com

"Your relationship with yourself sets the tone for every other relationship you have."